GOD'S FAVOR

Experiencing the Life God Wants You to Have

GARY WILKERSON

Chosen

a division of Baker Publishing Group
Minneapolis, Minnesota

Published by Chosen Books
11400 Hampshire Avenue South
Bloomington, Minnesota 55438
www.chosenbooks.com

Chosen Books is a division of
Baker Publishing Group, Grand Rapids, Michigan

Printed in the United States of America

ISBN 978-0-8007-9913-7

Library of Congress Cataloging-in-Publication Control Number: 2018040983

In some of the author's stories, the names and identifying details of certain individuals have been changed to protect their privacy.

Cover design by Darren Welch Design

19 20 21 22 23 24 25   7 6 5 4 3 2 1

"I have known Gary for his entire life, and I am so grateful for how God continues to use him for His glory. You will see Gary's tremendous passion for Jesus in *God's Favor*. Gary's pastor's heart comes through as he confidently and clearly shows how God wants to shower us with His favor, presence, grace, hope and kindness."

Nicky Cruz, evangelist and author

"I have known Gary Wilkerson for almost 25 years, and in the last few I have had the pleasure of traveling to many places and ministering with him. Gary has found something of God that is quite enviable. He has found not only a depth of Christ's love for himself but also a love from God that freely flows through him to others. In other words, he has discovered God's favor. I have witnessed the tears of joy, release and healing flowing down the cheeks of waiters and strangers as Gary speaks and prays with them. Let the words of this book touch your life in the same way."

Carter Conlon, senior pastor, Times Square Church, New York City

"Using examples from Scripture and life, Gary takes us on a journey to understanding the ultimate favor of God by encouraging us to walk in an attitude of favor to the revelation of God's ultimate favor, His very presence. A refreshing, recommended read!"

Jerry Nance, Ph.D., president and CEO, Global Teen Challenge

"Gary Wilkerson has been a dear friend for decades. What you are reading is not something worked out at a desk but something lived out in real life. What Gary writes he believes, and what Gary believes becomes part of his everyday life. What makes *God's Favor* an exciting read is that it's personal. Gary tells his story. It's not easy to read at times, but God's favor seems to always come through. *God's Favor* is refreshingly honest, scripturally insightful and constantly challenging. On these pages you will find favor when it seems there is none in sight."

Tim Dilena, lead pastor, Our Savior's Church, Lafayette

Having just celebrated forty years of what I believe to be the best marriage ever, I could not be more thankful for God's favor in sending me the most amazing, beautiful, lovely, and God-pursuing woman imaginable. I know God's favor in a richer way because you, Kelly, are in my life. Looking forward to 2050 together at ninety-two!

Contents

Foreword

Having been best friends with David Wilkerson for almost forty years, I knew his son Gary as a child. I know him now as a mentor. And I hear both voices through the pages of this book. It is more than powerful.

The search for purpose in life is embedded in the very core of human nature. Ultimate dignity and peace of mind come from attaining one's purpose for living. Most people, consciously or subconsciously, search for purpose their entire lives without finding it. It is like looking for love in all the wrong places. No level of success or fame or family or accumulated wealth can fully quench the human search for purpose.

Our search for joy and purpose is simplified by understanding almighty God as the holy Trinity—God the Father, God the Son and God the Holy Spirit—while we ourselves are body, soul and spirit. While our body feels pain and our soul experiences happiness, the fulfillment of joy and purpose in our lives is possible only when our spirit is in alignment with God's Holy Spirit.

And guess what? Searching for God's purpose for your life is not scriptural. God does not have one purpose for you and another one for Himself. He has but one purpose: to seek and save the lost. That is why He promises in Romans 8:28 to make everything in your life work together for good when you live your life for His purpose.

Gary explains that this is the sweet spot with God, when even the little things and bad things serve to fulfill God's purpose. When things go south, know that God is up to something! He is putting you in the middle of an opportunity to lead someone—or maybe lots of someones—closer to Him. And their redemption is far more important than your temporary inconvenience or lifelong challenge.

This is where the favor of God takes over. When you live your life for God's purpose, you live in His promise to make everything in your life work for good. This is when wholehearted, unwavering faith begins, and all the blessings that come with it. His favor is without limit, into the smallest areas of your life.

And there is more! In his last chapter, Gary takes us from God's unlimited favor in the smallest of things into God's ultimate favor that surpasses all things. You will find it hard not to moved to tears as Gary opens your eyes to the ultimate reward for living your life in *God's Favor*.

Barry Meguiar, president, Meguiar's Car Wax;
founder and president, IgniteAmerica
and Revival Outside the Walls

Introduction

We hear a lot about the favor of God these days. That's a good thing. Without the Lord's favor, we would not be able to breathe, stand or find true life anywhere. Our loving, compassionate God looks to bless us with His amazing favor.

But today the teaching of favor is being twisted by some. They use it as a means to gain material, physical and emotional blessings from God. That's tragic, because it reduces the Lord to just another American commodity. They tell you to invest a little church attendance here, sow a bit of financial seed there, claim the power of your tongue to confess your way into the life you dream of, and—boom!—you're favored.

That isn't God's way. He cares for us much more than that. If we get everything we dream of, that's not favor; that's lust. So what does it mean, in actual terms, to receive God's favor?

Ultimately, true favor isn't found in tangible blessings themselves. It's found in the One who does the blessing, our loving heavenly Father. Seeking Him, not things, is the hunger that dwells at the core of every human heart. We were made to find our life in Him. And God is jealous, in a righteous way. He won't allow Himself to be used as a means of fulfilling our lusts and self-gain. In fact, He will destroy all the idols we set up in our hearts so that He alone stands as our greatest desire.

This doesn't mean we shouldn't want to see God's blessings flow in our lives. Out of His loving grace and kindness, our Father delights in giving good gifts to His children. Just because some leaders have twisted biblical doctrines in the so-called prosperity movement doesn't mean the idea of God's favor should be thrown out. Rather, it should be rescued.

That's where pastors, teachers, counselors and parents come in. In our daily work, we see God's heart delighting in His people. He longs to demonstrate His good news in our everyday lives by showering us with His undeserved favor. He does this not because I "claim" what is mine as His child, nor because I give tithes and offerings, but because He is amazingly good.

We can trust in His goodness even when our children run away, when our marriage is failing, when our medical report is troubling, and when our soul is in despair. God's favor is with us through all of our struggles. And as we trust Him through every difficulty, we find that He leads us into greater favor than we could have imagined.

As we explore God's Word on the subject, you'll discover that His favor works in essentially two ways. First, our heavenly Father favors us with the nearness of His presence through our stormy times, commanding the winds and waves inside us to cease. I've learned a lot about God's love this way. It's a form of favor no Christian can do without.

The second way He favors us is through His tangible blessings—with power to rescue us, heal us and provide for us. I love testifying about how God has favored me this way.

He saved one of my sons from drug addiction and brought him to a renewed, deeply blessed life. That son is now happily married and serving Jesus. The Lord also healed my body after a car crash literally broke my back. That healing required surgery and a long recovery. Sometimes that's how blessings come to us—through hardships. Yet it's also how we learn that God's favor is with us in our trials. He not only healed my back but gave me a spiritual backbone, a Holy Ghost confidence that declares, "No matter what I may face, it is well with my soul. My Redeemer lives."

So, first, there's God's assuring presence, and second, there are His tangible blessings. Both are forms of His favor. And both are needed. To want only personal blessings of physical and material well-being is to limit the Lord. I believe it also grieves His heart. Yet to limit Him only to spiritual favor goes to the other extreme, denying God's role as a caring father who provides for our physical and material needs.

If I could only have one form of favor, it would always be God and His presence alone. I thank the Lord for His goodness, that in His great love He chooses to add the second form of favor: healing our bodies, saving marriages and families, providing for all our needs and lavishing His love on us, along with many things we don't deserve. Thank God He gives us both!

I pray this book will create a hunger in you for the ultimate favor of God's presence. And may it prepare your heart to receive His many blessings with joy and thankfulness. He looks to bless His people, and once you know you're in His favor, your life will never be the same.

PART I

GOD'S PART

*Blessing Us
with His Favor*

1

You Are Blessed, Not Cursed

Why God's Favor Has Never Left You

As a pastor for over three decades, I've done a lot of counseling. It's one of the roles I've enjoyed most as a minister of God's Word. I love addressing people's questions about the Lord and His ways. I've found over the years that His Word is faithful to address any dilemma of life, no matter how daunting or difficult. Almost always the answer has to do with God's goodness.

That was the case with a young man who showed up at my office one day in tears. "I lost my temper with my wife," he said, adding, with self-contempt, *"again."* It had happened many times before, he admitted: a sudden outburst, an exchange of angry words and in the end, a walkout. The young man had promised God it wouldn't happen anymore. But it did happen. And it kept happening—again and again and again.

As he poured out his heart I realized I was listening to an utterly broken man. He had struggled with anger his whole life, he told me. He tried for years to overcome it, but now he was afraid he had been overwhelmed one too many times. I saw the fear in his eyes; it was as if he sensed he had crossed a line and could never go back.

"I've blown it," he said. "I think I've ruined my marriage. I might even lose my family." He started weeping. Then he spoke the words he probably feared most. "I've lost any favor I might have had with God. His presence is gone from me completely."

I've met a lot of Christians who live with fears like this young husband's. Many devoted people of God believe their heavenly Father loves them and has showered them with the favor of His grace. But there's a side of their lives they feel is unworthy of God's favor. They're convinced that all the blessings they enjoy come from the Lord, but then they try to partition off the part of their lives that's marked by failure. Like Adam after the Fall, they want to cover their shame from God's gaze.

This is the dilemma of so many devoted followers of Jesus today. They have been deeply touched by God's grace. Yet despite years of battling to gain victory over their failures, they're still overwhelmed by their weaknesses. After a while, they begin to assume they have lost God's favor—forever.

I talk to these people wherever I go, and many end up telling me about a lifelong struggle they have had. They speak of the weight of their countless failures, which only continues to build up over time. Or they mention a specific burden they have carried in secret over the years or a fear they could never put behind them. In each case, the result is the same: After a while, their mindset of ongoing struggle begins to define their walk with God. Worse, it comes to define their view of God. Somehow, they become convinced that God isn't willing to help them overcome.

At some point, these precious people give up on believing they could ever have a fulfilling life in God. They abandon trying to find His purpose for their existence beyond tithes and church attendance. Sadly, today, they no longer believe they're a worthy witness of God, whom they know to be holy and good.

A lot of Christians have simply given up hope. Have you? Or has someone dear to you? Maybe you have a struggle of some kind you've never been able to shake. It may not be as severe as this young man's, or it may be similar. Perhaps it's worse. Regardless of the scale of your struggle, maybe you've been left wondering, "Can I really find joy in the Christian life? Where is Jesus' victory on the cross for me? Will I ever know it, or will I be caught up in this ongoing struggle forever? When will I know true freedom in Christ, rather than constant guilt and shame? When will I finally know what it means to have the abundant life Jesus talked about? Where has His favor gone?"

As I counsel people, I get absolutely blessed to see someone set free by Christ's good news. Suddenly, they become fully aligned with His purposes for them—and they come alive. After years of carrying an impossible burden, they're finally able to enjoy life. Nothing satisfies like the sight of someone who's been spiritually crippled finally getting healed. They spring forward from their despair with newfound hope, joy and faith. For them, it's a beginning glimmer of the promise of abundant life Jesus offers.

Yet seeing this happen doesn't usually come easily. The conflicts we each face every day are serious, because the challenges

of life in a fallen world never stop. And our trials are compli-
cated by the enemy of our souls, Satan, who works constantly
to obscure God's work in our lives. At any given time, even the
most devoted Christian can find himself or herself teetering
on the brink of despair and unbelief.

**Our deepest trials can send even the strongest,
most mature faith into turmoil.**

I can relate. At various times, I've had my own dark thoughts,
the kind that try to convince me I'm more cursed than blessed.

After our first child, Ashley, was born, my wife, Kelly, got
pregnant with our second child. We learned the baby was
a girl, and both of us did a little dance. "How perfect!" we
thought. "A younger sister for our strapping little boy."

But after eight months Kelly noticed the baby had stopped
kicking inside. We tried not to be alarmed and instead turned
to prayer. We trusted in God's goodness, believing He'd protect our child in the womb. But then came the sonogram
and other tests, and our deepest fears were confirmed. Our
baby had died.

By that time in my life I had been a pastor for over a de-
cade. I thought I knew God's precious grace inside and out.
But grief is a powerful force, especially when it's regarding a
child, and I absorbed our terrible loss in my own sorrowful
way. The first thought that came to me was the biblical story
of David, who sired a son who died shortly after birth. When
David learned the newborn's life was in jeopardy, he spent
seven days in agonizing prayer for him, pleading, "Lord, keep
my child safe. Don't let him die." But eventually the baby
did die.

Scripture tells us that King David caused his child's death
by his own grievous sins. When I reread that story that's

exactly where I went with my own grief. In my clouded, darkened frame of mind, I wondered what sort of sin I committed that might have caused our child to die. Though I had not committed adultery or murder, as David had, I was living in fear of condemnation. I prayed, "Lord, did my sinful thoughts make this happen? My laziness? My covetousness? My lust? What did I do that might have brought this to pass?" Our grief can be so overwhelming it sends us to places as dark as that.

Thankfully, by the powerful light of God's grace, the pain of my grief eventually began to subside, and my thoughts about it all became clearer. I thank the Lord that happened for me. I tasted His favor in a dark place, and it pulled me from the mental quagmire I was in. He did this for me by opening my eyes to the full power of a single verse of Scripture:

> But Christ has rescued us from the curse pronounced by the law. When he was hung on the cross, he took upon himself the curse for our wrongdoing. For it is written in the Scriptures, "Cursed is everyone who is hung on a tree."
>
> Galatians 3:13

Twenty years later, this powerful truth is still with me. I turn to it regularly, along with the other powerful truths of God's Word, as I counsel His people. Its sustaining power enables me to extend the same life to people like the distraught young husband who sat in my office despairing over his sin. As I shared it with him, I saw hope planted. His healing began.

Jesus' amazing work on the cross has rescued us from any possibility of a curse in all dimensions of life.

21

I have to ask you, What made you open this book? Maybe you saw *favor* in the title and you reached for it with one of two motives: You wonder whether you have God's favor in your life, or you seek God's favor because you feel it's missing. Either of these motivations is a good one. The favor of God is something we're all meant to enjoy, and He wants everyone who follows Him to seek it and know it.

Now, let me ask another question: favored or cursed? Which best describes your mindset from day to day? Many Christians don't know how to answer this because they don't know they're missing God's favor. Or, if they do, they don't think they deserve it. They feel more cursed than blessed. How do you feel? Are you walking in the favor of God, or does it seem like you're watching others enjoy the blessings of His favor, just out of reach of having it yourself? Do you know it's for you, or do you, like the young husband, feel bogged down by struggle and anguish?

Today, as I read Galatians 3:13, I come close to tears, especially as I think about the scores of Christians who have endured so much inner anguish. For some, having an embattled mind is a way of life. Somehow they have come to believe God is poised over them with a hammer, ready to beat them to the ground with any misstep. They have become so mired in their struggle that they have forgotten or lost sight of the favor God has promised to them as adopted sons and daughters. They have come to believe that God can't or won't be able to look past their sin.

So, how does a holy God view a young husband who struggles terribly with his temper? What happens to the righteous wrath directed at this man's sin? Christ's gospel answers us clearly: It all goes to Jesus. He took upon Himself all judgment for our sin—that's the curse aspect of the Law.

Christ paid the penalty for it—all of it. That young husband may still have to deal with the consequences and relational impact of his sin. But his sin is nailed to the cross. Jesus paid the price for his sin—and ours—in full.

The implications of this are absolutely profound. Two things leap out immediately.

First, it means we can't be cursed. Christ's perfect sacrifice won't allow it. Nothing can diminish the full, complete impact of the work He has done for us on the cross.

Second, it means that as God's children we live and move in a continual state of blessing. Because Christ has wiped out every curse, God's favor is on our lives. Each of us is the apple of His eye, His favored one, His blessed child. It doesn't matter how fierce our daily struggle may be. No weapon can ever prosper against this powerful truth.

We see these truths confirmed even in the Old Testament. Isaiah 53 famously prophesies about the suffering servant who would bear the punishment for our sin:

> All of us, like sheep, have strayed away. We have left God's paths to follow our own. Yet the Lord laid on him the sins of us all. . . . And because of his experience, my righteous servant will make it possible for many to be counted righteous, for he will bear all their sins.
>
> vv. 6, 11

Every sin, failure and shortcoming we could ever imagine is covered under Jesus' glorious work.

Some Christians see Christ's work for them on the cross as the promise of a clean slate but nothing more. These precious people believe God forgives them, but they don't believe their lives are blessed again until they spend a certain amount

vithout struggling. It's as if they're on probation.
ik, "I haven't had my same dark struggle for a week
st be back in God's favor." Then a setback occurs,
and the cycle begins again.

So, what's wrong with this picture? It's a deadening, re-petitive cycle that eventually kills the spirit. Here is the truth that's missing on this merry-go-round of despair: Christ's work for us does more than pronounce forgiveness. Isaiah 53:5 tells us it heals us, making us not only clean but whole: "He was pierced for our rebellion, crushed for our sins. *He was beaten so we could be whole. He was whipped so we could be healed*" (emphasis added).

The word for *healed* in this verse indicates more than physical healing of the body. It speaks of spiritual and rela-tional well-being, restoration of mind and soul, and a state of health relating to all parts of life. God's healing favor applies to troubled marriages and broken relationships as well as bruised minds and hearts. He covers it all.

Again, I think of the troubled young husband. To be sure, he has some faithful work to do to see Christ's victory over his temper. But even in his angriest moments this man has not been forsaken by God. On the contrary, God is on his side, and his family's, to keep bringing healing and even blessing to their home. As you'll find throughout this book, that's God's desire for all of us: to know the fullest blessings of His amazing favor. And those blessings reach the furthest depths of our lives.

**Deep down, many of us suspect there's a
catch to God's promise of favor.**

For those who know the Bible well, it's easy to get preoc-cupied with the two sides of God's promised favor mentioned

24

in Deuteronomy 28. For many Christians, it's a passage that's more troubling than encouraging.

As Israel was poised to enter the Promised Land, God prompted Moses to give them a two-part message. The first part was, in essence, "Obey God and your life will be blessed. If you walk in His Word you'll see blessings on your crops, your villages, your families—everything you touch" (see Deuteronomy 28:1–14). What an encouraging word! It's all about God's blessings and the abundant life He intends for us.

Then came the second half of the message, which spoke of curses instead of blessings: "Likewise, if you do not obey God, you'll be cursed in your fields, your villages, your families, everything you put your hands to" (see Deuteronomy 28:15–68).

A lot of Christians read this chapter in the Bible and think, "My life falls more into the disobedient category. That's why my life isn't blessed. It's why I still struggle, why things don't go my way." They may not say it aloud, but at some deep level these Christians believe they're cursed in God's eyes.

That's not what this passage conveys at all. God's bottom line to His people was this: "I *want* to bless your life—your parenting, your work, your relationships, your community life. Stay in my Word, live the way I've prescribed for you, and you'll have a blessed life." Still, many read this chapter and think, "The moment I depart from God's commands, He automatically moves me to the cursed category."

But Moses knew God's message to Israel was good news, not bad. A few chapters later, he addressed each of Israel's individual tribes with specific words of awesome blessings:

> Let the tribe of Reuben live and not die out, though they are few in number. . . . Give [Judah] strength to defend their

25

cause. . . . Bless the ministry of the Levites, O Lord, and accept all the work of their hands. . . . The people of Benjamin are loved by the Lord and live in safety beside him. . . . O Naphtali, you are rich in favor and full of the Lord's blessings.

Deuteronomy 33:6, 7, 11, 12, 23

The list of blessings Moses spoke went on and on. And it wasn't because these tribes were perfect. They weren't!

Tell me, as you read this passage, do the words sound like threats? Do you picture a hammer being held over the people's heads? Of course not. Moses goes on to speak powerful words of blessing to all twelve tribes.

So what does this have to do with us today? Like Israel, we can be tempted to think of our life as continually cursed as we endure trial after trial. We might even be tempted to think we deserve our trials, that our sin has brought them on. And, yes, sin does have consequences, but it doesn't cause condemnation or a curse. Jesus already resolved that for us, once and for all.

You may ask, "But doesn't the Bible say God chastises those He loves?" I've heard this question from a lot of Christians. They say, "I agree that God favors us with His grace. But no Christian is free from God's discipline. Even the New Testament says He chastises those He loves." That's utterly true. But there's a vast gulf between our heavenly Father's loving discipline and the wrathful judgment of a curse.

My dad demonstrated this difference to me when I was a boy. At times he spanked me for acting up or disobeying my mom. But afterward he always made me go into the backyard and play football with him. That always seemed like a worse punishment, because I was still mad at him for

26

spanking me. But it was a wise strategy on Dad's part. He made sure we never went back into the house until I had a genuine smile on my face from the joy of playing with my father. It taught me that he loved me and that his correction was part of his love.

That's exactly the kind of love that's behind all our Father's discipline. If we're heading down a wrong path that leads to destruction, He won't hesitate to grab us by the collar and say, "No, I won't let you do that. I love you too much."

Yet God's favor isn't limited to the protection of an earthly father. It does something more that's absolutely mind-blowing: God's favor sets us free completely from the curse of darkness, because He paid the penalty for our sin in full.

Today when any Christ-follower reads the blessings and curses in Deuteronomy 28, he is given an important truth. Yes, God is holy and requires holiness of His people. But here is His promise—His favor—to you through the cross: "I'll take on the cursed part. And you take on the blessed part. I'll take on your sin, and you take on My righteousness."

Think about what an incredible promise this is. As we consider what Jesus did, and does, for us, it becomes impossible to live in defeat. Do you live as if you're cursed, doomed, having no future? If so, I fear you've been persuaded by a lie, one that's meant to derail you from the awesome truth of what Jesus has done for you.

If you think you'll never be an overcomer, I have good news for you. Scores of Christians fear they have to strive for every blessing. And the pressure of that burden fills their lives with stress. They don't understand that they're already blessed.

You may say, "I'm only being a realist. My life has never been any different, and I don't ever expect it to be. Isaiah 53 has no effect on me." Friend, those aren't the words of a realist; they're the words of a doubter. It's a refusal to accept what Christ has already done for you.

You see, there's a mental discipline that's required of us if we're going to live in God's favor. By *discipline*, I don't mean some rigid work apart from God's grace. I'm talking about communion with the Holy Spirit, the Comforter, who brings to our remembrance all truth about our Savior. We need that discipline for a crucial reason: It's because we have an enemy, Satan, who opposes us—an adversary who constantly fires lies meant to derail us from the awesome truth of what Jesus has done.

If you need encouragement about your endless cycle of failure, consider this: God actually uses our personal struggles and long, difficult seasons to prepare us to receive the blessings of His favor.

This powerful truth is demonstrated in the life of every faithful figure in the Bible. In fact, the lives of the first Christians demonstrated it. No generation in church history ever had it harder than the early believers. With everything they faced, including bloody, horrifying persecution, the first-century followers of Christ had every reason to doubt God. But they knew a deeper reality than their outward circumstances.

You're probably familiar with the scene at Pentecost: Under the anointing of the Holy Spirit, the apostle Peter stood up and preached to a massive crowd with three thousand people getting saved on the spot. Immediately those converts of different tongues, ethnicities and nationalities began to love each other. It changed their lives completely, to the point that they lived and worshiped together, sharing all things in common. The Bible says there was not a need among them. And all of this happened in the shadow of a cruel and brutal Roman occupation.

Then persecution followed, and it was severe. Yet the church's numbers increased daily because of the joy and love they shared despite their sufferings (see Acts 2:47). Then, when persecution intensified, multitudes of Christians met their deaths. Many believers ended up fleeing Jerusalem, scattering in all directions. Imagine the losses they endured: homes, businesses, land, possessions, family members. I think of the world's many refugees today—driven from home by wars, terrorism and persecution—trudging hundreds of miles carrying their children and their possessions in a backpack. Watching them, I better understand what the early Christians went through.

Yet in spite of these unimaginable hardships, the first-century believers were a powerful witness wherever they landed. Scripture tells us Barnabas was awed by what he saw in the scattered church: "When he arrived [in Antioch] and saw this evidence of God's blessing, he was filled with joy, and he encouraged the believers to stay true to the Lord" (Acts 11:23).

Despite their grievous circumstances, and being seen as the offscouring of the world, the early Christians became missionaries of blessing.

Here is the core of the favored life we have in Christ: His favor is with us in everything, even when our struggle persists over a long period of time.

Throughout the world we see the curse of sin warping humankind and wreaking chaos. But we who know Jesus have been set free from the curse of darkness—all because He paid the penalty. Indeed, the good news of Jesus brings life and blessing wherever it's demonstrated in word and deed.

I witnessed tenacious belief and dedicated, courageous action from a couple whose faith was challenged by an undisputable reality. When their son was in second grade, a group of school officials, including a psychologist, came to them with dispiriting news. They declared that the boy had a severe learning disability. The best he could ever hope to achieve in life was the lowliest rung of manual work. They advised the parents to remove the boy from school and start training him so maybe he could eventually learn a trade.

The couple listened intently. They were in full reality about their son's condition. Yet they weren't in denial when they told the officials, "Thank you for your insights and concern. We respect everything you have to say. But we don't believe that's God's plan for our child."

The actions they took to spare their son the fate described by experts were costly. Instead of pulling him out of school, they kept him in classes and then spent long hours tutoring and encouraging him despite discouraging results. They constantly told him, "We believe in you."

Years later, what God implanted in their hearts came into full reality. The parents watched as their son crossed his high school's stage to accept a diploma. He then went to college, where he received all As. Today he pastors a thriving church.

Friend, your marriage isn't cursed. Your finances aren't cursed. Your health isn't cursed. Because of Jesus, you live in a permanent state of blessing. So, it doesn't matter what your outward circumstances may be; you're walking in God's favor, which was secured for you by Christ. That is your reality. His Word says so. And, just as He did with the first-century Church and with the parents of a child with a disability, Jesus has made you His missionary of blessing.

I can assure you of this about God's favor: "No eye has seen, no ear has heard, and no mind has imagined what God has prepared for those who love him" (1 Corinthians 2:9). If you're willing to hope for that, read on.

2

Your Season of Increase

Releasing a Harvest of His Favor

Life can be difficult, with long seasons of struggle. And for that reason, our trust in God's love for us has to be increased continually. That's why in my decades as a pastor I've grown to appreciate more and more the wisdom of Paul, the church's first great over-shepherd. One of the most important lessons I've learned from his example is this: God wants His shepherds to build up His people, not to tear them down.

Many of us start out strong in our faith. Early in our walk with the Lord we see victory after victory. It's as if the kingdom of heaven has opened up to us personally, and everything we experience is fueled by His storehouse of heavenly treasure. Yet as time goes on, the victories we enjoy can seem harder won and fewer and farther between. That naturally brings up questions—even doubts—about our life in Christ. We wonder, "What happened to God's glorious presence in my life? Is His favor still with me? Or did I do something wrong to make it go away?"

There are seasons in all our lives when we feel stuck, static and stranded on a spiritual plateau with nothing to show for our faith. We tell ourselves, "I'm doing all the things I'm supposed to do. I've prayed. I've believed. I've invested my whole life in my walk with Jesus. But it doesn't feel like I'm advancing anymore. Somehow, I'm in a strange season when nothing seems to change—and I can't see a way forward. There has got to be more to the Christian life than what I'm living. I have to see greater victory."

Whenever I hear these thoughts from Christians, I think of a farmer who plants and tends his fields faithfully but never sees a yield. This farmer works hard plowing and turning the soil, and he has the sunshine and rain on his side. But nothing he sows sprouts or grows; he never sees any promising buds or spritely green shoots, no signs of life. Anyone in his situation might wonder, "Season after season I invest all my time and energy. But I never see an increase. I sow faithfully, but for some reason I'm unable to reap. I've done all I can, with nothing to show for my labors. What more could I possibly do?"

I have a message for everyone who feels stuck on this kind of middle ground, discouraged and not knowing what else to do. Read on. The Lord will encourage you, straight from the Scriptures.

A lot of us don't feel cursed, but we never feel truly blessed either.

Many Christians don't think God is against them, but they can't seem to find the blessing of His favor. They haven't given up believing their heavenly Father is out for their good—that He wants to heal, strengthen, encourage and transform their lives. Yet they don't know where to turn to find the abundant life He promises.

Maybe this issue shows up in their marriage. Their relationship with their spouse isn't bad, but it's also not what they hoped for. A husband comes home from work emotionally drained from his demanding job and immediately zones out watching television. As his wife prepares dinner, she longs for just a few minutes of conversation to remind them of their sacred bond, that they're not just going through the motions. Or, maybe a wife comes home from her job, her mind churning with all the chores that need to be done after dinner, while her husband wishes for just one moment of genuine connection.

Many Christian spouses have sowed faithfully into their marriage for years, but they don't feel they reap from their efforts, never seeing an increase from what they have invested. They don't blame their spouse, because both seem stuck somehow. They're stranded in a kind of neutral territory, unable to find a way to grow. Their common cry is, "I know the Lord is good, that God's design for the marital bond is supposed to be fulfilling. So why isn't there more in this for me?"

I assure you, God cares about your marriage. He doesn't want to see you stuck, no matter what difficulties you're facing, whether dwindling finances, a demanding job, troubled children or something else. He wants all the gifts and experiences He has given you to come to full fruition, blooming into a lush, full-bodied harvest. In fact, every promise in His Word reveals His desire to see you enter a season of increase. Let me show you how.

God actually uses our difficulties to bring about an amazing harvest.

I know what it's like to desperately "pray for rain." One of the greatest agonies of my life was when two of my boys were involved in drugs. It was a prolonged agony, lasting for years. At one point, one of our addicted, prodigal sons even ended up homeless. Kelly and I prayed for them for years, never knowing the right thing to do. Sometimes we intervened aggressively, and at other times we pulled back, because we saw that our efforts only pushed them away. We never knew the right way to help them. Their trials went on for years, and it tore us up inside.

It's a terribly helpless feeling not to be able to help your children, especially when you see their futures—and possibly even their lives—at stake. Kelly and I tried everything we could think of. But no effort we came up with seemed to bear fruit.

Do you struggle with your children? A lot of Christian parents today see their kids moving so far away from God that they think it's hopeless to keep praying. But I can tell you from experience that there's hope. The Lord rescued our sons. It took a long time, and we continually had to surrender them to the Lord. Yet, thank God, no situation is ever lost to Him. And here's why.

Remember the lesson from the previous chapter: Because Jesus removed every curse, we live in a constant state of blessing. God's desire at all times is to bring healing and joy to our family. Yet He doesn't do it by waving a magic wand over all our difficulties. No, His promise is to be with us *through* our difficulties. All the while, He is building in us a faith that's as strong during our hardships as in those times when we can see and feel His blessing.

My father's life offers a powerful example. He went through a heartrending situation with his brother, Jerry, when they were both young fathers. Dad was a well-known evangelist with success as a bestselling author. At the same time, my uncle Jerry was spiraling into alcoholism, and eventually he ended up leaving his family. When my siblings and I were little, we remember every night being tucked into bed by Dad and praying with him for Uncle Jerry.

Years later my uncle came back to Jesus—miraculously, at one of my dad's evangelistic crusades. It took a long time to get to that night, and when it happened, it wasn't just my uncle who changed; Dad changed, too. He recognized how he had neglected his own brother while he ministered to crowds of thousands. Their relationship was different after that. Uncle Jerry even came to work in my dad's ministry. Talk about a season of increase for our family. Uncle Jerry's return wasn't just about deliverance for one but healing for all. That's the kind of amazing harvest only God can bring about through our deepest sorrows and hardships.

Do you believe He is looking out for you, caring for you and demonstrating His concern for you, despite your struggle? If you need further proof, consider His words to Israel: "I will cause you to be inhabited as in your former times, and will do more good to you than ever before" (Ezekiel 36:11 ESV). God is telling us, "If you think I blessed you in your early years as a Christian, you haven't seen anything yet. I'm going to do more good for you than you've ever known. You have coming a season of increase that you never could have planned for."

The Bible is filled with figures from history who seemed permanently stuck, unable to find God's increase for their lives. Moses had a great passion to see the children of Israel set free from their bondage in Egypt. He was raised in Pharaoh's house with a top education and superior skills. Yet in a moment of vengeful passion, Moses killed a cruel Egyptian slave driver who was abusing a slave. He had to flee into the desert—an exile that lasted for decades.

At one time Moses was a royal prince, but he ended up tending sheep for his father-in-law. Stuck in a dusty, barren wilderness year after year, Moses must have been tempted to give up completely on God's plan for him. He had to wonder, "Lord, after all Your preparation, all Your promises, there has to be more for me than this. I want my life to count for something. Most of all, I want to see Your people set free!"

A similar bewilderment fell upon Elijah's life. The mighty prophet singlehandedly slew four hundred prophets of the god Baal in a literal mountaintop victory. But as Elijah enjoyed his great victory in the Lord's name, an enraged Queen Jezebel sent a stampeding force to take the prophet's life. Suddenly, Elijah was on the run, just as Moses was. He ended up hiding in a cave, exhausted to the point that he couldn't even feed himself. He had to be brought food by birds. At one time a hero, Elijah was now a marked man with a bounty on his head throughout the land. Discouraged and depressed, Elijah was stuck in a moment with seemingly no way out.

Some Christians read these stories and think, *That's just the way God is. He makes life hard for His people. You see it in the Bible, and you see it in your friends' lives, too. Let's face it: Life with God is full of hardship.* I want to ask such Christians, "Have you read the end of these stories—how Moses became Israel's deliverer?" God worked amazing wonders through Moses on Israel's behalf. Thousands of years later, even the secular culture uses phrases like *promised land* and *parting the Red Sea*—references to miracles associated with Moses, whose life God had powerfully redeemed.

Have you considered how Elijah miraculously ended a years-long drought in Israel? Even Jesus refers to Elijah's amazing story in the gospels. And James writes of God's Spirit moving powerfully in the prophet's life after the attack from Jezebel:

> Elijah was a man with a nature like ours, and he prayed fervently that it might not rain, and for three years and six months it did not rain on the earth. Then he prayed again, and heaven gave rain, and the earth bore its fruit.
>
> James 5:17–18 ESV

James is saying, "Elijah was as vulnerable to despair and depression as the rest of us. He agonized over his failures and defeats. Yet this same man actually made the rain stop and then start again. Anybody who sets his or her face to seek the Lord in all things is going to have power with God."

What an amazing picture of the Lord's power in our lives. He is able to move us through our most desperate trials into victory. These stories tell us that no season of stagnation lasts forever and that God eventually turns our difficulties into a season of increase. Thankfully, Moses and Elijah understood this—and they never gave up hope.

God knows the end of your story, too. The Lord is writing your story even now, in the midst of your trial. That's what the author of Hebrews means when he writes that God is the "author and finisher" of our faith (Hebrews 12:2 KJV). And the end of the story is always this: *God is for you.* He is on your side, caring for you, looking out for you and demonstrating His concern for you, no matter what your circumstances tell you.

We can never neglect Ezekiel's reminder, especially in our season of difficulty: "I will cause you to be inhabited as in your former times, and will do more good to you than ever before" (Ezekiel 36:11 ESV). When Ezekiel spoke these words, Israel was living in a kind of middle ground. They weren't sinning outright, but they weren't fully serving Him as they had in past generations. At times in their history they had been captivated by idols or captured by hostile nations. Yet even in those times God never cursed them, saying, "I've had enough of your merry-go-round of sin. I'm done trying to work with you. You've finally frustrated me too much. Away with you. You're a hopeless case." On the contrary, God instructed Ezekiel to tell the people, "Hold on. Turn your hearts back to Me. You're going to see more of My blessing in your lives than you've ever known before."

Jesus gives us a powerful picture of God's desire to bless us with increase.

"Hear then the parable of the sower. . . . As for what was sown on good soil, this is the one who hears the word and understands it. He indeed bears fruit and yields, in one case *a hundredfold, in another sixty, and in another thirty.*"

Matthew 13:18, 23 ESV, emphasis added

Imagine you're a first-century Israelite, and you're hearing this for the first time. Many of the people listening to Jesus on that occasion were actually farmers. Any one of them would have rejoiced to get a full acre's yield out of an acre's worth of seed they sowed. That would make for a full harvest, and it was real cause for rejoicing. Yet Jesus was telling them, "Imagine waking up and finding that your seed spread beyond what you planted. It fell between the rows you planted. It leaked out of your seed sack on the way home. It trailed behind you on the path up to your farmhouse. All along the way, seed fell and grew into a bountiful harvest beyond what you hoped—thirty times, sixty times, even a hundred times more. Can you imagine that?"

No, they couldn't. It was utterly impossible. That was the point Jesus was trying to get across. Our heavenly Father has a multifold increase in mind for us all, a harvest that only He can produce. And He uses the very seeds of our lives—the good times and the bad, the triumphs and the struggles—to bring about His harvest. That is His way, and it is glorious.

The key to this passage is whether or not we will hear His word and cling to it through our bad times as well as the good. God is increasing your influence and significance, and that isn't based on your circumstances, whether pleasant or challenging. Both work for God's greater good in causing your life to be an ever-increasing blessing on the world around you: "As for what was sowed on good soil, this is the one who hears the word and understands it. He indeed bears fruit and yields" (Matthew 13:23 ESV).

Jesus' message to us is clear: Your Father wants a lot for you—much more than you could ever imagine!

Sometimes life deals us harsh lessons that we wrongly attribute to God. It's hard for a lot of Christians to imagine their heavenly Father offering His overabundant favor to them. That's especially true if they grew up with a harsh parent. They see God as a kind of unapproachable ogre, somebody who's ready to criticize or rebuff them any time He's near. And so they tend to keep a low profile and not ask for much. They might not admit it to their fellow Christians, but deep down they content themselves with just making it to heaven.

That isn't God's design for any of His precious children. That's why even timid, cringing Christians eventually grow discontent as they go on with the Lord. They know by the

Spirit's groaning within them that God has something more for their lives, despite their cripplingly inaccurate image of God.

I have my own experience of a misguided image of the heavenly Father. My own father wasn't a harsh parent. He could be gruff at times, especially when he was overworked, but he was also an affectionate dad. Even so, all it takes is one isolated incident from childhood to form an inner conviction that distorts our view of God.

I wasn't the kind of kid who asked for much. In fact, I rarely asked my dad for anything. When my siblings and I were young, Dad traveled so much conducting evangelistic crusades that we were happy just to have him home. Yet while he was away I consoled myself by getting absorbed in comic books. On the back cover of every issue was an advertisement for some kind of toy, and the one that caught my eye was a Civil War set. It had dozens of soldiers and horses and cannons, mesmerizing me with the dazzling world it promised. The set cost a few dollars more than I had access to, but I knew who did have access: my dad. To this day I've never met anyone more generous, and back then he always carried around bills to give away when he encountered anyone in need.

At that age, I saw my dad as an easy mark. So, one afternoon while he was relaxing on the patio, I asked him, "Dad, you know I never ask you for much—" and I showed him the advertisement with the toy set. He must have been under some great pressure at that moment, because I wasn't ready for his response. He grabbed the comic book out of my hand and bellowed, "Why do you keep asking me for stuff? I give you everything you need, and then you want more!"

I was shocked. His reaction was completely out of character for him. I quickly backed away, and for the rest of the day I gave him a wide berth. Yet deep down I blamed myself for triggering his anger. That's what a tender young conscience will do, especially one that never asks for much. I also formed a deep conviction that day, one that I held on to for a long time: Don't ask for anything. It could be dangerous. And you aren't worthy to receive it.

A lot of us project this same misguided conviction onto God. Some of us have been so blessed by the Lord that we feel timid about asking Him for more. In fact, some Christians end up creating a pharisaical code of humility that states, "It's prideful to ask for more than the Lord wants to give me." Yet this approach is rooted more in cringing fear than a true fruit of the Spirit.

All of this does God a great disservice, because He is nothing like what our approach to Him suggests. That's the point of Christ's parables when we come to our Father the way a farmer does who says, "I just want an acre's worth of crops," God responds, "You aren't asking for enough. I want to give you a hundredfold!"

That's exactly the point of a powerful passage in Isaiah:

> I said, "I have labored in vain; I have spent my strength for nothing and vanity; yet surely my right is with the LORD, and my recompense with my God." . . . [The Lord] says: "It is too light a thing that you should be my servant to raise up the tribes of Jacob and to bring back the preserved of Israel; I will make you as a light for the nations, that my salvation may reach to the end of the earth."
>
> Isaiah 49:4, 6 ESV

In other words, "Isaiah, you ask simply for My broken people to be restored. But I say I'll make My people a powerful witness to all the nations of the world."

That's the God we serve, the One who takes the meager acre of our lives and does something amazing with it. We cringe before Him because of our lack, our brokenness and our meagerness, and yet He says that's exactly the stuff He wants to use to bring forth a hundredfold harvest for His kingdom. We think, *Lord, I'm just an average person who has so many faults.* But He says to us the same thing He told a cringing Moses: "Don't tell Me your faults. I already know them all. And I have a plan for your life that's beyond anything you can imagine. While you're battling your difficult circumstance, I'm busy making you a light to the nations."

There's a powerful reason God wants us to ask, seek and knock. Our heavenly Father wants to open the windows of heaven to us so His name will be glorified as never before. David addresses this when he declares, "You will increase my greatness" (Psalm 71:21 ESV). Anyone might read these words as boastful or even greedy. But David had something holy in mind. He had already conquered his enemies in amazing fashion, but he knew that each additional victory was another testimony to God's power on His people's behalf. That's why he wrote, "Not to us, O LORD, not to us, but to your name give glory, for the sake of your steadfast love and your faithfulness!" (Psalm 115:1 ESV).

Indeed, throughout his life David never settled for less, saying, "I've accomplished enough. God has done plenty through me. My legacy is set firmly in stone." Instead, David wrote, "May the LORD give you increase, you and your children!" (Psalm 115:14 ESV). He reasoned, "This is no time to slow down my requests of the Lord. Oh, God, pass these blessings and more down to my children and to their children. I want my ceiling to be their floor. May Your glory increase with every generation that knows You!"

Paul points to an even more specific reason for God's promise of increase: "He who supplies seed to the sower and bread for food will supply and multiply your seed for sowing and increase the harvest of your righteousness" (2 Corinthians 9:10 ESV). Here is the harvest God is after: righteousness that spreads a hundredfold from its humble beginnings.

Friend, that is His design for your life. And it all starts with another kind of increase, one that Paul prays for us all: "May the Lord make you increase and abound in love for one another and *for all*" (1 Thessalonians 3:12 ESV, emphasis added). This increase of love is meant for our spouse, our children and our fellow Christians. Yet when Paul adds we're to "abound in love . . . for all," it extends to our boss, our coworkers, our neighbors and the people we meet at the mall, the coffee shop and the grocery store. The Lord has an increase of His glory in mind, and He aims to accomplish it through your life and mine.

Can you imagine your marriage being a hundredfold better? God extends that to you.

Can you imagine your relationship with a sour coworker being a hundred times better? God holds out that promise to you as well.

Can you picture yourself sharing the powerful love of God with that kiosk clerk at the mall? That's exactly the kind of harvest He has in mind for you.

To accomplish this, He asks us to change our view of His love for us. I have a testimony of my own when it comes to this. You see, my father eventually surprised me by giving me that Civil War set. When it arrived in the mail I was awed on several levels. First, despite my fear over his difficult outburst, I never doubted my dad's love for me. And second, I saw the great delight on his face as I opened the package and began playing. His expression erased any lingering fear I may have had about approaching him for good gifts, and it cemented for me the awe that an unexpected gift from our heavenly Father can bring.

We're all going to have trying days. But we can never doubt the amazing love that our Father promises is ours. I'm sure my dad never doubted God's ability to perform miracles after my alcoholic uncle Jerry appeared at a David Wilkerson crusade. Likewise, friend, have no doubt about your Father's love for you, no matter what trials you face. Right now, He is writing a story of increase for you—a very different kind of season, all to His great glory.

3

Favor Follows You

His Favor Is Always at Work for You

Favor follows you.

How do you respond to this statement? It isn't just a phrase I say to encourage you. It's a fact based on passage after passage of Scripture. Yet I have found that very few of us in Christ's body live as if this fact is true. God's favor does follow us—through every day of our lives, no matter what a given day may bring. It's important to know this, because as long as we live in this broken, fallen world we're never going to be problem free.

In the previous chapter, I mentioned problems in marriages and with children. But what about physical or mental sufferings? Some Christians struggle with depression. They wonder if their cloud will ever lift so they can sense God's sweet favor again. Others endure excruciating physical pain. Right now, our nation is undergoing a serious opioid crisis with an alarming overdose casualty rate, and it's being fueled mostly by average people who get addicted trying to find relief from excruciating physical pain.

No matter what our problem, some of us struggle to believe our situation will ever get better. You might answer my opening question this way: "Favor follows me? It feels more like disfavor. God's favor is the last thing I see in my day-to-day life. I can hardly believe all the problems piling up around me. I never thought the Christian life would look like this. In fact, I don't feel like I have a witness anymore. My life feels more like a disgrace than a testimony. I'll be honest; there are times I'm ashamed to reveal to strangers that I'm a Christian."

I can guarantee you no Christian ever pictured himself being in seasons like this. No one ever imagined their hardships would outweigh the comfort or power they feel from God. Yet Peter tells us we aren't to think of such trials as unusual:

> Beloved, do not be surprised at the fiery trial when it comes upon you to test you, as though something strange were happening to you. But rejoice insofar as you share Christ's sufferings, that you may also rejoice and be glad when his glory is revealed.
>
> 1 Peter 4:12–13 ESV

Peter offers a reminder of a theme from the last chapter. That is, if you're in the midst of an excruciating season of life, hold on. Don't give up hope, because the Lord isn't finished with your story. His glory has yet to be revealed in it.

You may think you're alone in your predicament, that you have brought disgrace to His name. But Peter speaks to multitudes of Jesus followers when he says that all along God has been storing up blessings for you, to show you favor you never dreamed of. He states clearly that God's glory is going to be revealed through your trial, and the time to rejoice over that is today.

That's the word I wish to bring to a struggling single mom I know. Her husband abandoned her and their two children, and now bills are beginning to pile up. She doesn't know where to turn. What's she supposed to think when she reads this chapter's opening statement, "Favor follows you"? To her, the opposite seems true. She is struggling just to survive, watching her children suffer, one need after another rushing at her without relief. As things turn from dim to dark to bleak in her world, it's hard for her to imagine anything wonderful ever happening again. There's a huge disparity between what she knows of her loving, faithful God and the very real circumstance she faces. What does that do to her faith?

In seasons of struggle, the root of our dilemma is a matter of faith. We can't see God at work. Yet the Bible tells us that's exactly what the Lord is doing in our crisis.

> No eye has seen, no ear has heard, and no mind has imagined what God has prepared for those who love him.
>
> 1 Corinthians 2:9

Few of us associate this verse with our seasons of struggle. Instead, we read it the way a child anticipates an approaching birthday: "God has something great prepared for me? Awesome!" Yet embedded in this verse is an incredible truth about our discouraging times: God is at work for us, always. While we struggle through difficult days, He is constantly at work building, creating, moving and changing things on our behalf. It's all part of His amazing favor, a favor that follows us continually, no matter what our circumstance.

I want to convey two urgent truths to every Christian who identifies with the struggling single mom. First, hold on. God is actually storing up great blessings for you. Your day is coming. He has your appointed time in mind. And, second, we can never forget that Satan constantly seeks to steal from us. The enemy of our souls attacks most fiercely when we're undergoing stressful trials. That's when our capacity for hope is most vulnerable. And that's just what the devil is looking to steal from us—our hope. If he can rob us of that, he can steal our future, the blessed destiny that God is at work shaping for us.

Yet here is another amazing fact about God's favor: Even if our hope has been robbed, the Bible tells us God wins it back for us. And not only that, He multiplies it. The oldest book of the Bible, Job, demonstrates this most famously, but other passages point it out as well. For instance, in Old Testament times, if a thief was caught stealing something, he had to replace it sevenfold. In the New Testament, God promises to do even more, replacing things one hundredfold. In short, His favor goes beyond restorative justice, spilling over into boundless grace. And that amazing grace is the power behind all of God's favor.

Even if we can't see God at work, our heavenly Father has been actively working since our ordeal began, storing up His appointed blessings for us.

The Bible tells us in passage after passage this is exactly what God is doing at all times—working to change things on our behalf. Jeremiah 29:11 (ESV) tells us, "For I know the plans I have for you, declares the LORD, plans for welfare and not for evil, to give you a future and a hope." As Paul says, our minds can't fathom what the Lord is preparing for all of us who love Him (see 1 Corinthians 2:9). And David testifies, "How abundant are the good things that you have stored up for those who fear you" (Psalm 31:19 NIV).

You may feel like the opposite of these passages is happening, that everything you cherish is being drained away. But all along God is working to bring about the blessing He has prepared for you.

I want to borrow a brief illustration I once heard that has stayed with me powerfully. Let's say you've just secured a dream job and you show up for work on Monday ready to dive in. Then when Friday comes, your paycheck doesn't arrive. You think, *Hmm, maybe I'm being paid monthly.* But at the end of the month, you aren't paid, either. You begin to wonder if you aren't measuring up to the job. You think you've lost the boss's favor. You begin obsessing over anything you might have done wrong.

This continues for another couple of months, and your spirits sag further and further. What you don't know is that on the coming Friday your boss won't only pay you three months' wages; he'll give you *thirty years'* wages. It's an amount you never would have imagined coming your way—and one you could never truly earn. When that happens you think, *Whoa, I don't deserve this. It's an outrageous amount. I could work the rest of my days and never earn all of what I've been given!*

Yet that's the very nature of God's grace when He blesses us. We may feel like things are in decline, but all the while the Lord is planning a blessing that's meant to take us by surprise and humble us through His mercy.

During the barren months and seasons of your life, your mind may tell you one thing. But think about what's actually happening. God isn't idly neglecting you. He is thinking of you the whole time, creating a blessing you never could've dreamed would happen.

Here's something else to consider. The blessing we're looking for as God's children isn't primarily material or physical. It's God Himself. It's more of His presence, greater depth built into our trust and faith, and greater peace and joy in our turbulent times. That kind of intimate knowledge comes only through difficult, trying seasons. In His omniscience, God knows those things couldn't come to us any other way. What seemed like a withholding of favor was in reality a blessing on many levels at once—a work of far greater favor. We're blessed not just on a physical or material plane but in our strength of heart.

Often, that doesn't occur to us when we're in the midst of our struggle. Instead, we're left wondering whether God will ever answer our prayers. In fact, sometimes after we pray, things seem to get worse instead of better. And as we confront even more oncoming trials, our hope in God's promises falls by the wayside. We wonder, "I don't see any reality of God in this. Why should I keep believing?"

I want to tell every fellow Christian that the Lord isn't idle in your life. Even when things seem dead and hopeless, you can be assured His favor hasn't been lifted from you. On the contrary, He is on the job achieving His greatest kingdom work yet. What seems like a lack of favor today will prove He was at work behind the scenes all along, storing up great benefits for you.

Here is something we don't hear taught much about God's favor: He uses our difficult seasons to prepare us for His blessings. That's right—God's preparation for us to receive His blessings doesn't happen before or after our difficult season.

It happens *during* our time of trial. While we think He has abandoned us, He is actually at work within us, preparing our hearts.

Abram provides a wonderful example of this (see Genesis 13–14). God led him and his family to a new land, where they were blessed immensely. In fact, their herds quickly outgrew the land they owned. So Abram took his nephew Lot aside and said, "Look at all this land surrounding us. There's so much abundance. Why don't we stake it out and divide it up so our blessings will keep growing? Just pick out which direction you'd like to go, Lot. You can have whichever half of the land you want and take half of our herds to graze there."

Lot saw that one side of the land was lush and green, favored with rain and flowing water. The other side was rockier and more arid, with hardly any watering holes. Naturally, Lot chose the lush side of the land.

So, do you think Abram was disappointed over that? Did he ever question himself, *Why did I let this happen? Life would have been so much easier if I'd kept the lush land for myself. I could have let young Lot develop the drier, rougher land.*

I don't think that ever crossed Abram's mind. Surely, he knew which side of the land was better when he offered it to Lot. Yet Abram also knew something that was more important to him than land. It was that God assigns favor according to His own thoughts, not according to our planning, strategizing or understanding.

As it turned out, Abram's herds continued multiplying, even in the dry land. Why? You could say Abram brought favor to an unfavored land. That kind of thing happens only by God's determination. Meanwhile, the more "favored" region that Lot chose was ravaged by war and strife between the ruling kings there. In fact, eventually, several of them banded together to take Lot and his family captive. Abram, the man in the "unfavored" land, had to rescue him.

Abram didn't need the lusher, greener land, because he knew the nature of the God who owned it all—and he trusted in God's faithfulness. The outward appearance of the land meant nothing to him. He knew God's favor was accumulating for him all along. **Abram's story shows us that our own direction in life doesn't determine our destiny. God does.**

I know a lot of faithful Christians who are convinced of something God never told them—that they have been disqualified forever from a life of favor. They think, *I've blown it. I made a terrible decision earlier in my life, and it changed everything. Now I'll never know God's favor again. My path is determined forever.*

For some it was a bad business choice. For others it was their choice of spouse, and the marriage ended. For others it was an addiction or a lust that wrecked a blessed relationship or a fruitful career. So they think, *That's it. I ruined it. Nothing can change the course for me.* Their way of thinking begins to lean more toward expecting curses than blessings.

But nothing could be further from God's truth—or from His plan for your life. It doesn't matter how you arrived at your current circumstance. God wants to bring favor to your marriage *now*, blessing to your work *now*, richness to your family bonds *now*, joy to your friendships *now* and courage to your walk with Him *now*.

You may be tempted to change courses drastically, to make something new happen to distance you from your past mistakes. Maybe you're compelled to turn your life in a different direction, to move on your own to correct things. But that may not be God's plan for you. It *is* His way to bring you out of the wreckage of your sin and failure and to make His glorious light shine in your life again.

Let me point out here, there's nothing wrong with making wise choices for change. In fact, I would encourage those kinds of choices, especially when someone is entangled in an abusive or potentially dangerous situation. But often I see Christians leaving difficult situations just because it's the easiest answer.

Here's the problem with that: When you run from a difficulty, you end up running away from the blessing God has for you on the other side of it. What's more, you may be running from one problem to a worse one—say, from a tension-filled marriage to a relationship that will prove to be ten times harder.

You may feel your life is in total misery, with no possibility of redemption. But I can tell you this for sure: God wants to show you His favor right where you are, in your present circumstance. It doesn't matter how you got there. He is changing things already. In fact, if you were able to see this, you wouldn't feel like giving up. And you wouldn't feel like running from your problem. Instead, you would know the best is just ahead for you.

Jacob's story proves that when you're a child of God, it doesn't matter how hopeless your circumstance looks. His favor is going to rain on you. Jacob agreed to work for crooked Laban for seven years to be able to marry his daughter, Rachel (see Genesis 29). But when those seven years were up, Laban gave Jacob a different daughter to marry, Leah. He forced Jacob to work another seven years before giving him Rachel, the daughter he had wanted to marry fourteen years earlier.

That was a long time to wait for the one he loved, but things later proved even worse for Jacob during his years under Laban's thumb. Laban tricked Jacob in all kinds of ways, changing his wages and squeezing him to get all he could from his son-in-law's labors. Jacob knew he could never overcome the bondage he was entangled in. But he knew God could, and Jacob trusted the Lord's word to him that he was favored. It led him to make an outlandish suggestion to his father-in-law.

"Instead of giving me these miniscule wages," he said, "why not let me have any sheep that are born spotted?" Spotted sheep were incredibly rare. But for Jacob, having livestock of his own was the only way he saw out of his impoverished life.

Laban clearly saw his advantage in the deal Jacob was offering, so he quickly agreed to it. Then to his surprise, every lamb that was born came out spotted. Laban quickly broke off the agreement. So now Jacob proposed, "Okay, all the white or spotted sheep are yours. But if any come out striped, let me have those." Whoever heard of striped sheep? Again, Laban agreed. But as you might guess, every sheep was born striped.

Despite his own flaws—and his own crookedness at times—Jacob knew the fantastic grace of walking in God's favor. He could endure every treachery by Laban because he was secure in his knowledge that God was for him. Jacob knew his day would come, and it did. Later, he became known as Israel, God's chosen beloved.

I've learned through forty years of ministry that the more difficult the trial, the greater the reward at the end of it.

God can be at work behind the scenes, even when there's an appearance of tragedy. I have a friend whose life became a modern-day version of Job's. Deeply blessed, he was shocked as his life blew up almost overnight. The wife he loved and cherished had an affair, breaking his heart. Despite his pain, my friend loved her and was determined to repair the marriage. He worked hard to make that happen, but his wife chose a different path, leaving him for the other man. Within a few weeks, he lost his well-paying job. That caused him to lose his house. The losses meant his wife would get custody of their children.

In the midst of it all, he came to me totally distressed. "I'm out of work and homeless," he said. "I've lost my family, everything I loved. My life will never be the same." He seemed completely out of hope.

If ever there were someone whose life appeared to be in disfavor, it was my friend. We both knew nothing could ever make the situation right, to repair the blessed life he once had. Divorce is always harmful and hurtful.

Yet God did something supernatural for my friend. A few years later he met a beautiful, loving, godly woman. She loved him and became the delight of his life. When they got married I saw my friend become the happiest man I'd ever seen. Around that time, he got a job with a growing company and worked his way up to an executive position. It was a beautiful, amazing thing to behold.

When things looked bleak, beyond all hope, my friend could have easily chosen a different direction for his life. Instead, at the very time he felt God was absent, something in his heart told him otherwise—and he held on. When it looked as if all favor was gone, that his broken life would never be whole again, he knew in his heart, "My Redeemer lives." Somehow, he trusted that during his most painful time, God was accumulating for him a great harvest in His storehouse. He eventually saw that when he thought he had lost God's favor completely, favor actually followed him.

Maybe you're in a dark hour, perhaps the darkest you've ever known. The things pressing you down haven't changed for years. Yet the reality is, God's favor follows you. No bad decision you ever made can hold Him back from blessing you as He desires. He is your Savior and also your Redeemer, the One who resurrects beauty from ashes.

He is with you in your circumstance, building up your blessings in His amazing storehouse. And you can know that the longer you endure your storm, the greater His supply for you. His purpose for you isn't finished, and His favor surrounds you: "We know that God causes everything to work together for the good of those who love God and are called according to his purpose for them" (Romans 8:28).

PART II

OUR
PART

*To Rest
in His Favor*

4

Conquering Cynicism

The Mental Discipline of Knowing God's Favor

I have a friend I've known for over twenty years, a guy who once ran an amazing ministry. When he started out, people came to Christ wherever he preached. Doors opened quickly for him to speak around the country, and as his outreach grew, Christians saw his impact for the gospel. Suddenly people were lining up to give generously toward his work.

Eventually my friend was able to buy an office building for the growing support staff he needed. God was clearly blessing what this friend did, and we all rejoiced to see his tremendous impact for the gospel. What this friend experienced was a joy any minister would relish: to be able to speak for God and see His work transform hearts and lives.

Then, at some point, the ministry stalled for no clear reason. My friend got fewer and fewer invitations to speak. The people who supported him began to drop off. Eventually he had to lay off staff members and cut back his outreach. And the more he prayed about the obstacles he faced, the less his prayers seemed to be answered.

We all have to realize that any blessed work we're handed is always God's, never ours. Whether or not you serve God in a formal ministry, any servant of His has to acknowledge up front that the Lord builds and the Lord brings down. It's His work, not mine. I have to be faithful to do what He puts in front of me, no matter how small or large. He is the force behind it all.

I'm sad to say, this wasn't the attitude of my friend. His disappointment over the loss of his ministry was so heavy he couldn't get past it. A seed of bitterness took root, and the shift in him was clear to everybody.

I saw the changes in him every time we met. All of his talk about God was negative, and he made cutting remarks about people. It was so uncharacteristic that I had a hard time believing this was the same friend. He once believed God for great things and saw them come to pass. Now he quickly shut down any mention of God. No matter how much grace I showed him, he was committed to cynicism. He eventually became very hard to be around.

There's no other way to put it: My friend's faith trajectory was dark. He had moved away from faith, confidence and boldness to fear, cowardice and withdrawal. He went from believing God for great things to not believing Him for anything at all. Finally, he was so discouraged and beaten down by his losses that he left ministry altogether.

Maybe you know people like my friend. They used to be hopeful, forward-looking, generous toward others, trusting of God's sovereignty. But something in their lives took a turn, and suddenly they became negative. They're not just down on themselves but eager to spread discouragement to others. If you tell them how God has blessed someone, they react with an array of negative answers: "Sure, but do you know the other part of the story?" "He hasn't taken his hard knocks yet. If you're serious about God, you end up taking a lot of beatings." "The person you're talking about is still immature in their Christian walk. Wait till they run into a brick wall. Then you'll see what they're really made of."

We've all had disappointments in life to varying degrees, and it's easy to let our lingering questions turn into seeds of bitterness. Maybe the fiery faith you once had was diminished by a disappointment. Your confidence in God's favor took a hard knock and hasn't recovered. Now, as you look around at others who still seem to enjoy His favor, you feel a growing bitterness start to take root.

Friend, you don't have to succumb to that. Thank God, His Word gives us powerful examples of people who resisted cynicism. They all faced the same temptations toward bitterness we face today, and by God's powerful grace they conquered them.

The story of Elisha and the widow he helped is a brilliant example of how cynicism can be conquered. Scripture says Elisha received a "double portion" of God's blessing. This simply means he was a man of unrelenting faith. And he set that faith into action when he met a widow who'd been dealt some of life's cruelest blows. This woman had lost her husband, the love of her life, and suddenly she had to provide for herself and two sons (see 2 Kings 4). Yet his death left her so deep in growing debt that it would take her several lifetimes to pay it all back.

As a pastor I've counseled a lot of people who faced mountains of debt. Most of them didn't bring this on themselves. Sometimes it happened because they lost their job, or their medical bills started piling up. They got behind on payments, and soon they were drowning in a never-ending credit plunge. That's when the collectors' calls started coming.

I don't know if you've ever experienced it, but calls from creditors are a psychological plague. They come at all times of day—early in the morning, at dinnertime, and into the evening. They carry harsh messages and threats that the whole family hears on the answering machine. Being in that situation is a nightmare that happens to many good people, who can't believe it's happening to them. They look back and wonder how this ever came to pass in their lives. And they see no way out of their dilemma.

As discouraging as this can be, it's nothing compared to the threats this widow received. If she didn't pay her bills, she was going to lose more than her property. According to the law of the day, her creditors had the right to enslave her sons.

Talk about an opportunity for bitterness to take root. The widow had already seen hardship beyond her imagining, and the frightening news about her sons' potential enslavement could have frozen her heart with cynicism. She might have turned to Elisha in anger, railing, "I prayed for my husband's healing, but he died. I prayed for God to help me find a way out of debt, but it has grown so huge I can't pay it all back. Now my sons are about to become somebody's slaves. Tell me, Elisha, why should I cry out to God? He hasn't answered me for anything else. Why should I possibly believe He's going to rescue my sons from this fate? Go ahead, pray if you want—as if that's going to work."

Cynicism is a know-it-all, seen-it-all attitude that cuts off belief in God's abilities on our behalf.

Cynicism creates a joking spirit that accuses God about His goodness. A lot of cynical Christians think they're wiser than the rest of us. Their attitude conveys a superiority that says, "You're just naïve. If you knew what I knew, you wouldn't be so hopeful. It's frivolous to say, 'I believe God is moving in great ways.' How can you possibly know whether He's moving at all?"

We don't know whether the Israelite widow had that kind of cynicism. If she did, Elisha stopped her from any opportunity to express it with his gentle offer to help. He immediately saw that she and her sons were hungry and had no food. Elisha's belief in the Lord's goodness led to an amazing intervention. Scripture describes their exchange:

> "What can I do to help you?" Elisha asked. "Tell me, what do you have in the house?"
>
> "Nothing at all, except a flask of olive oil," she replied.
>
> And Elisha said, "Borrow as many empty jars as you can from your friends and neighbors. Then go into your house with your sons and shut the door behind you. Pour olive oil from your flask into the jars, setting each one aside when it is filled."
>
> 2 Kings 4:2–4

Elisha's suggestion may have sounded a little crazy to the widow. Was she really supposed to stockpile empty jars while angry creditors were on their way to take her sons? A cynic would have scoffed at this, saying, "Sorry, Elisha. You know what I've been through. Why put me through some crazy exercise? I tell you what. You fill this flask of oil first. Then we'll see about whether I'll go around to my neighbors begging for jars like a madwoman."

A remark like that can seem like simply the offhand reaction of a hurting person. But in reality, it's a lot more serious than that. It's an accusation against God's goodness. And it can have terrible consequences.

Cynicism shuts all doors to God's work.

If we aren't willing to move forward in faith, we cut off any hope for God to move in our lives. Fortunately, that's not what happened here. Elisha's faith evidently stirred this widow, because

> She did as she was told. Her sons kept bringing jars to her, and she filled one after another. Soon every container was full to the brim!
>
> "Bring me another jar," she said to one of her sons.
>
> "There aren't any more!" he told her. And then the olive oil stopped flowing.
>
> 2 Kings 4:5–6

What a scene. As the oil kept increasing, the widow quickly ran out of jars to contain it. So she directed her sons to go into town and find more jars. They kept racing to their neighbors, borrowing jars to bring home, and racing back out again. Each time they entered the house, they saw another stack of oil-filled jars reaching toward the ceiling. Finally they returned, telling their mom, "We've knocked on every door. We've asked every neighbor. We've sought out every merchant. You have all the jars we could possibly find in this town. There aren't any more left!"

Picture their excitement as the destitute house was suddenly filled with marvelous, miraculous oil. When they realized the great value of what they had, they must have jumped up and down crying, "Look at what God can do! Hallelujah, Lord!"

When the work was finally finished, the widow raced to tell Elisha about the miracle. Elisha's response may seem calm on the page, but this prophet of God had to be over-joyed to tell the widow what God's plan had been all along: "When she told the man of God [Elisha] what had happened, he said to her, 'Now sell the olive oil and pay your debts, and you and your sons can live on what is left over'" (v. 7).

It was a miraculous intervention. Just like that, the widow's fortunes and her family's fate were changed forever by God's amazing provision. Yet this isn't what the story is about, not entirely. Rather, it's a picture of God's goodness and abundance, and His desire to bless us with it. You see, oil is a powerful symbol in Scripture representing the Lord's overflowing blessings. The widow's story is a picture of God's endless, overflowing ability to care for His people in their most troubling crises.

Today, because of Jesus, God is present with us even more than with this widow. Christ is our double portion, and He has promised to pour out His Spirit on us, just as He poured oil from heaven to bless this widow. In His goodness, He looks to fill us abundantly with all the faith, confidence and boldness we need to face any trial. When we find ourselves at our lowest, we're to cling to Him in hope. Even a mustard seed of faith is able to bring down a tower of cynicism.

God has set an appointed time when He'll move for us, but we can block that movement with cynicism.

You may wonder, as I do, "What if the widow hadn't gathered up all those jars? Would she have missed out on her miraculous deliverance?" Matthew's gospel gives us the answer: "[Jesus] did only a few miracles there because of their unbelief" (Matthew 13:58). What an astounding statement. The miracles that the Creator Lord of the universe performed were fewer than they could have been, all because of the people's unbelief.

You can almost see the cynicism dripping from people's words as they dismissed Jesus:

> He returned to Nazareth, his hometown. When he taught there in the synagogue, everyone was amazed and said, "Where does he get this wisdom and the power to do miracles?" Then they scoffed, "He's just the carpenter's son, and we know Mary, his mother, and his brothers—James, Joseph, Simon, and Judas. All his sisters live right here among us. Where did he learn all these things?" And they were deeply offended and refused to believe in him.
>
> Matthew 13:54–57

This passage makes clear that Jesus is never the problem whenever we face trials. The problem is our cynicism.

It also tells us a lot about where the church stands today when it comes to believing the Lord is at work for us. Entire denominations have built their theology around the idea that God isn't active in people's lives, that He doesn't move in the world anymore. If Elisha were to go to them today, these leaders would look at each other, grin, offer a friendly pat on the prophet's shoulder and say, "It all sounds great, Elisha. But that kind of thing doesn't fly here. God worked that way back in the day, but not anymore. Why don't you take your message to the church down the street? We're just fine without it."

I don't question these denominations' sincerity or experience. But their theology reduces God's living, breathing Word to a mere moral document. They boil it down to a list of dos and don'ts, a guide for living. And they restrict the Holy Spirit to a voice we hear only at the point of our conversion but not afterward. It denies God's living presence in the world.

What a terrible misrepresentation of our loving, compassionate, incarnate God. He stands ready to pour on us His oil of abundance at all times. And He proves this again and again, both in Scripture and in the restored lives of our hope-filled brothers and sisters in Christ. That's a blessed hope we don't dare give up.

I witnessed the importance of maintaining hope when one of my sons fell in love. My son Evan tried to regain hope after a series of failed dating relationships. He was tired of trying to make things work only to see them end in disaster. So, he committed it all into the Lord's hands. "God, I only want your will," he prayed.

About that time, a young woman began attending our church—and Evan was drawn to her. Normally, the pain of a badly bruised heart might have made him hesitant. But having committed his all to God, he trusted that the stirrings might be real—and might lead to something good. He had faith that God would lead his steps.

Evan decided to approach her at church, and as they talked, he felt a deep connection between them. He immediately had feelings for her, and the more they talked, Evan realized he was "borderline in love."

Shortly after that, Evan learned she was about to take a trip to see her family in New Mexico, where she grew up. He wanted to be careful to pursue her in a way that was honest and honored the Lord. So, he decided to write her a letter to let her know his feelings.

She left on her trip—and Evan heard nothing from her. No text, no email, nothing about the letter where he poured out his heart. All communication stopped.

Evan started to worry. Had he been wrong to write her? With every silent day that passed, the old feelings of hope-lessness surfaced. Still, Evan clung to God. He got on his knees again.

"Lord, this is going nowhere," he prayed. "If it isn't your will for us to be together, then don't let her contact me. But if it is your will, I pray that I would hear from her. A—"

Before Evan could say "Amen," his phone rang. He looked down at the screen—and it was her.

Faith surged in Evan's heart. To him, it was a clear answer from a faithful God. My son doesn't believe in setting out fleeces—actions that test God to see whether He'll answer. Evan believed the timing of that call was the Lord telling him, "You asked me to be in control of this. And I am."

But there were still hurdles ahead. Her communication to Evan was shaky. And she didn't return his feelings. Then Evan saw on Facebook that she was hanging out with an old love interest in her hometown.

It shook him. So, he called her. "It's nothing," she assured him. But the familiar feelings of failure crept in, and he lost it. He messaged her on Facebook—and it was harsh: "I don't want to see you again," he wrote.

Evan was brokenhearted. And he projected all his past experiences onto her. It didn't take him long to realize what he did was wrong. But the damage was irreparable. He anguished over it.

Then he remembered the timing of the phone call and how God touched him through that. He shook his head at how he was acting now. "Lord, this doesn't make sense," he prayed. "You kept Your promise to me. I made it impossible. But Your will makes it possible for us to be together."

Eventually, there was another phone call, and the couple talked. "I don't believe those things you said," she told him. "I think God has something for us."

Through it all—even his own failure—Evan trusted that God was faithful. I'm so proud that my son didn't give in to cynicism. Instead, he gave birth to hope that led to true blessing. Some time ago, I officiated at this amazing couple's wedding. A wonderful young woman named Carmen now graces our family.

Cynicism is contagious.

When God chose Moses to lead His people to freedom, He did several things to build Moses' confidence in the face of that task. He spoke to Moses audibly. He showed him a sign through a burning bush. He gave him the words needed to convince Israel they would be delivered from Pharaoh. Imagine Moses' excitement at this news. I can picture him rejoicing, "After all these years in bondage, God is moving on our behalf. He is about to set us free!"

So what happened when Moses delivered the message? Israel's elders scoffed at Moses, saying, "Our people have slaved in this iron furnace for over four hundred years. We've cried out to God for generations with no answer. Now you say God spoke to you, and He is on the move? Sorry, Moses, but how do you expect us to take you seriously?"

Moses' response was telling. He turned to God and asked, "Lord, if my own people don't believe me, how will Pharaoh react? I don't even speak well. I stutter when I talk. You picked the wrong guy for this." He had approached the Israelites with a fired-up faith, but now he faltered from doubt because he absorbed the people's cynicism.

What a terrible picture of how contagious cynicism can be. It happens in Christian families all the time. If kids don't see their parents believing God, they're tempted to give up believing, too. Then, to keep from despairing, they turn to a screen and enter a fantasy world, or to sex or drugs or other addictions.

Cynicism is also contagious in churches. When a congregation stops believing God is at work in the world, they turn from an intimate walk with Jesus and start to emphasize works or moralism. Yet all the while, God never stops calling them into the powerful, transformative work of His kingdom: "Hope deferred makes the heart sick, but a dream fulfilled is a tree of life" (Proverbs 13:12).

Thank God Moses didn't allow cynicism to stick. Instead, he offered his heart to God in faith. That led to one of the most powerful deliverances of a people in world history.

God knows your circumstances, and He is for you. Are you willing to move forward in faith to gather up jars for oil? Will you resist the contagion of our time and believe God is good? Will you accept that God's favor never leaves you, no matter how threatening your circumstance or how accusing your thoughts?

Join me in prayer to conquer the cynicism threatening so many followers of Jesus:

Lord, my faith barely registers anymore. But You have the power to take away my unbelief. Please stop the negative flow of thoughts through my mind. Stop me from using the caustic words I've grown used to saying. Help me to speak kindly and generously, believing in Your goodness. I offer my heart to You, to remove everything that hinders me. I've been blind to Your favor in my life. Please, restore my sight to Your goodness. I want to see You move mightily again.

5

Your Family's Greatest Season

Taking a Stand for Jesus
Can Change Things Forever

How do we change our family's destiny? Especially when those who came before us had a rocky history? Maybe your family has been broken by generations of dysfunction. Maybe it has been riven by strife, separation, addictions or abuse. If that's the case, you've probably wondered, "What can one person possibly do to turn all this around? What does it take to change things?"

Or maybe that isn't your family's history at all. Maybe your loved ones' story is a good one. You might have had a lot of ups and downs, but for the most part you see your family as blessed. If that's the case, then let me ask you a different question: How do you turn a good family into a great one? How do you ensure your family continues to stand as a living testimony to God's goodness, in spite of the difficulties you face?

How you pursue these questions has everything to do with entering the fullness of God's favor.

Your response to your family dynamic is important to how God shapes your family's destiny.

My father grew up in a Christian home that was very legalistic. The strain of Christianity his family took part in didn't allow people to have washing machines because it was thought to lead to laziness and sloth. Skirts had to fall to the ankle, and makeup was forbidden. Sports events were also off limits because they were considered worldly, not of eternal value.

Part of what informed this hyper-religious dynamic was the fear of a severely punitive God. If you sinned, you could be sure the Lord would find you out, expose you and punish you with awful consequences. With that sort of image of God, it was hard for a kid like my dad or his siblings to live with any sense of freedom. Sadly, they continually looked over their shoulders and wondered if something they were doing might be offending the Lord.

One day when my dad was in elementary school, he came home to an empty house. He looked into his pastor-father's study and saw his dad's clothes draped over the chair and his shoes on the floor. Then he went into his parents' bedroom and saw a dress and stockings lying across the bed. He went upstairs to his siblings' rooms—all empty, too. Why was everyone suddenly gone? Pondering it, my father panicked. He thought his family had been raptured by Jesus—and he was left behind!

He ran screaming through the house, scared out of his mind. That brought his parents running to him from wherever they'd been, asking what was wrong. When he explained, his parents didn't offer comfort. Instead, they used the moment as a lesson: "Think about what you just felt, David. That's what will happen to you if you don't live for the Lord."

My grandparents had good intentions, but they didn't recognize their need to break a crippling generational fear. Above everything else, my father and his siblings needed to know the Father's love for them beyond any fear that could be instilled in them. Instead, the family dynamic continued to revolve around a legalistic fear—and it caused different reactions in my father's siblings.

Dad himself desperately sought to please his father. I've already mentioned his middle brother, Jerry, struggling with alcoholism for a long period. Their oldest sister vacillated between agnosticism and atheism for decades. All of this happened despite the fact that they descended from a long line of ministry families that went back generations. My dad's father was a denominational leader over his region. And his father's father had been a well-known evangelist within the denomination.

My dad had great respect for his predecessors and was proud of the legacy passed down to him. He eagerly accepted the high calling he felt to continue that heritage. Yet Dad knew there was something fundamentally wrong in his family's dynamic. He knew things had to change. So, when he became a young pastor, he determined to free the people in his congregation from any legalistic heaviness, and he worked to be free of it himself.

I see now this became a lifelong pursuit for my father. It took him years and was a gradual process. Finally, in his sixties, he discovered the teaching of the New Covenant. He learned about Christ's full, complete accomplishments for our salvation and the Holy Spirit's ability to keep us. Yet even then he struggled against the legalistic impulses that were embedded in him through his family's influence. But God's grace won out.

Speaking for my own family, my children and grand-children, I couldn't be more grateful to my dad for the stand he took. He spent a lifetime wrestling with the vestiges of legalism in his own heart. And although his struggle affected my siblings and me somewhat, we grew up learning more about God's loving grace than about fear and performance. In short, Dad drew a line in the sand, saying, "Things change now with my family and me." And from that moment on, generations would see the benefit.

> **Your family's greatest season begins when one person takes a stand and says, "No more. Things change starting today."**

We see this biblical truth demonstrated in Jacob's family. Jacob had his own struggles with deceit in his early years, but that part of his character was redeemed by the Lord. Then, as his children grew, a terrible heritage began with Jacob's son Levi. Jacob's daughter Dinah was raped, and Levi and several of his brothers were enraged by the crime. They sought revenge, raiding the village where the rapists lived, and they slaughtered all the men there. When Jacob heard about this, he was furious at his offending sons.

> You have brought trouble on me by making me stink to the inhabitants of the land, the Canaanites and the Per-izzites. My numbers are few, and if they gather themselves against me and attack me, I shall be destroyed, both I and my household.
>
> Genesis 34:30 ESV

Evidently, Levi never departed from his violent ways, despite his father's displeasure. The stain on Levi's household lasted even to his father's deathbed. As Jacob said a final good-bye to each of his children, he blessed all of them except for Levi. Instead, he passed on a kind of curse to Levi's family, saying, "Cursed be their anger, for it is fierce, and their wrath, for it is cruel! I will divide them in Jacob and scatter them in Israel" (Genesis 49:5–7 ESV).

For centuries after this, the tribe of Levi isn't mentioned much in Scripture. It's likely the violent dynamic of the father got passed down through the generations. That's not hard for me to imagine. I think of how easily legalism was passed down in my family from generation to generation, acting as a kind of curse on the emotional and spiritual makeup of Wilkersons. That is, until my dad took a stand.

In the Levites' case, the day came when things changed for them. They took a stand that finally broke their family's odious legacy. Because of that critical decision, the family entered into a great blessing that lasted down through every generation.

It happened after Moses descended from the mountain where he met with the Lord. When he arrived at camp, he found the Israelites partying around the golden calf they'd made. He demanded, "'Who is on the LORD's side? Come to me.' And all the sons of Levi gathered around him" (Exodus 32:26 ESV).

That last verse may seem quiet on the page. But if you know the Levites' history to that point, you realize what a powerful move it was for them. With one resolute decision, centuries of sordid Levite history began to change. Moses recognized it and said, "Today you have been ordained for the service of the LORD, each one at the cost of his son and of his brother, so that he might bestow a blessing upon you this day" (Genesis 32:29 ESV).

Think about Moses' statement here. The Levites "ordained" for themselves a breakthrough and a blessing, all by stepping out and saying, "Change starts right here, right now." And what a turnaround it was. They became the priestly tribe of Israel, performing the rites associated with God's holiness.

God can do the same in your family. He did it in mine, and it has made all the difference. All it takes is one stand, and things can be transformed forever.

If you're from a broken family, you may fear the heritage passed down to you, wondering, "Will my marriage and kids manage to avoid being fractured the way my family of origin was?" As you look back over your family history, maybe you feel there's no way to break traits that seem like an inherited curse. It might be a tendency toward addiction. It might be anger or contentiousness. Or it might simply be a negative attitude or a cloud of fear about life in general.

I want to tell you about an amazing turnaround that birthed one of the most vibrant families in our church. Kelly and I adore this couple and their three wonderful children. The wife is active in our church in so many ways, and her husband is equally dynamic. I've rarely met anyone as energetic and full of joy. Yet if you knew this couple's history, you would never guess they would have the blessed family they have today.

We knew them for a while before we found out that the husband had one of the hardest family histories we'd ever heard of. His mother suffered severe mental difficulties, was constantly paranoid and threw wild fits of rage. She aimed a lot of her anger at her son, demeaning him and telling him he was worthless and hated. She once locked him in a closet and left him there all day long.

The boy's father owned a bar, and on most nights he came home drunk. He went into alcoholic rages and would strike his vulnerable little boy.

What a horrible home environment for any child. I can't imagine the untold damage all this did to our friend's tender young spirit.

Then, at age fifteen, this boy encountered Jesus. His parents didn't allow him to attend church, but he decided to go anyway. He often paid a price for that decision. But he had no regrets as he grew in his knowledge of his heavenly Father's love for him. And so, his long road to healing began.

Later, he met a wonderful woman, a hardworking, devoted lady who was employed by a large ministry. They got married, and this man grew healthier and healthier. Then they began having children, and that brought more and more joy to the family they were making.

As I look at our friend today, I'm amazed. His is so powerful a transformation that only God could have performed it. He is a living testimony of what the Lord can do for even the most damaged soul—that of a child with no advocate, no adult to care for him, and just the healing love of God. There was a time in his young life when every force conspired to drag him into permanent despair, but he stood up and said, "No, I've placed my hope in Jesus. I'm going to follow Him." The rest is history.

The blessed breakthrough didn't stop with him. The stand he took years ago has determined the direction of his family. His children aren't scarred by what could have been a heritage of trauma. Instead, like the Levites, he has been a missionary of God's blessing. The Lord's powerful grace over his life now blesses his family's future and erased what the enemy sought to steal from generations.

When I consider his story, I think of Joshua's challenge to Israel:

> If you refuse to serve the LORD, then choose today whom you will serve. Would you prefer the gods your ancestors served beyond the Euphrates? Or will it be the gods of the Amorites in whose land you now live? But as for me and my family, we will serve the LORD.
>
> Joshua 24:15

There's no need to despair over your family or your own brokenness. According to God's Word, and to testimonies like this man's, you can be the forerunner to a blessed generation.

There are vast numbers of families awaiting the kind of transformation Jesus desires to bring.

In his short story "The Capital of the World," Ernest Hemingway begins with the brief but compelling mention of a Madrid legend about a father and his son, Paco, that has since been expanded on. The tale goes that the two clashed all the time, with tensions rising by the day. Finally, there was a harsh exchange, and the father told the boy he no longer wanted him in their house. The son stormed out, swearing he'd never come back.

Once the father calmed down, he was heartbroken. He went out looking for his son but couldn't find him. Days passed, then weeks and months, with no sign of the boy. With every sunset the father agonized over another lost day with his son, longing to restore him to the family.

One day a neighbor told the father he had heard a rumor that the boy, Paco, was now living in Madrid. Immediately, the father set out for the city to find him. He searched for days, following every possible lead, but every day he came up empty. Finally, he began to believe it was useless.

He couldn't bear to go home without making one last-ditch effort to find his boy, however, so he decided to place an ad in Madrid's newspaper. It read simply, "Paco, this is your father. All is forgiven. Come home. I love you." A line was added asking the son to meet the father the following morning at the entrance to the newspaper building. If he didn't come, the father would know to give up his search and go home.

The next day the father walked to the newspaper building. When he arrived, there were eight hundred young men standing at the entrance. All were named Paco, and all had been estranged from their fathers—and hoped it was their father calling them to come home.

I believe that gracious pursuit is built into every father. Sons need to know their fathers love them and are proud of them. A young man's masculinity is formed primarily by how he thinks his dad perceives him. And the same dynamic exists between fathers and daughters. How he treats and speaks to her conveys something she needs to know about her femininity. This isn't to diminish the role of a mother. Of course, her words and attitude toward her kids are just as vital and central to their development. But for any of this to happen in a child's life—to see their spirit flourish—a parent has to take a stand. And sometimes that stand is one of forgiveness.

This legend tells us something profound about every human being: Deep within us is a desire to see our broken family restored by a grace that's beyond us. All it takes is one of us reaching out with Christ's forgiveness, and everything can change.

John 11 contains a famous story about a broken family that tried to change their destiny. Scripture doesn't tell us why two sisters, Martha and Mary, were in charge of their brother, Lazarus. Something must have happened to their parents. All we know is that the two women did their best to create a family dynamic that would help their brother navigate through life. Then a day came they hadn't expected. Lazarus got sick—so sick, in fact, it was clear he was dying.

The sisters turned to the only hope they knew: their friend Jesus. How did Christ respond? He delayed going to them. In fact, He waited so long that Lazarus ended up dying before Jesus arrived. The anguished, grieving sisters tried not to cast blame. But when Martha saw Jesus, she couldn't help saying, "Lord, if you had been here, my brother would not have died" (John 11:21 ESV).

Still, Martha trusted Jesus' ability to transform their tragedy. Even when it seemed beyond hope, she said to Him, "Even now I know that whatever you ask from God, God will give you" (v. 22 ESV). A few minutes later, her sister, Mary, came to Jesus expressing the same grief—and the same faith.

If the story stopped here, I wonder what many of us would think of Jesus. Picture how this story might be discussed on a daytime talk show: "Our mom and dad passed away tragically when we were still teenagers. Suddenly we had to provide for our younger brother. Life was hard, and we suffered a lot. Then our brother got sick. It looked like he was going to die, so we sent for our friend, who's known as the Great Physician. He works medical miracles for people. But when we called for Him, He didn't come."

At this point, I hear boos from the studio audience. "What an insensitive doctor!" they cry. "He could have changed everything for this family. But now they're broken beyond repair. Imagine the sad life those sisters have ahead of them!"

That's exactly the response some people have toward God when they consider their own tragic family history. They wonder, "God could have changed everything in my family's story. So what happened to His favor over us? I thought His Word promised we would be blessed, not cursed. Instead, we have to live through all this torment and pain. We've worked hard to overcome our tragic past. But we've been saddled with so many struggles we might never overcome them. Why would a loving God allow a situation like ours?"

When Jesus entered the sisters' story, however, a change began. When He first arrived, He was confronted by an entire community in anguish. Many on the scene wondered why this Messiah who could open the eyes of the blind couldn't be troubled to heal His sick friend Lazarus. But Jesus had already revealed to His disciples, "For your sake I am glad that I was not there, so that you may believe" (v. 15 ESV).

Then, to the astonishment of everyone, except maybe the sisters, Jesus prayed for Lazarus to rise from the dead.

> He cried out with a loud voice, "Lazarus, come out." The man who had died came out, his hands and feet bound with linen strips, and his face wrapped with a cloth.
>
> John 11:43–44 ESV

In one powerfully dramatic moment, everything changed. In a single instant—as two sisters expressed their precious faith despite their anguished grief—a family's destiny was transformed forever.

Even though he was raised from the dead, the work of Lazarus' healing wasn't quite finished. There's a further lesson for us in this story. Seeing Lazarus wrapped in graveclothes, Jesus said, "Unbind him, and let him go" (John 11:44 ESV). Sometimes it takes a while to unwrap ourselves from life's effects, which may still carry the stench of death. But the Holy Spirit gives us power to walk in newness of life. He is now in charge of our transformation. And He is telling us, "This is your divine moment. Everyone who takes a stand in My name, I will honor with the resurrection power of heaven."

Your changes may not be instantaneous. Like my father, you may have to wrestle out of the graveclothes of your past. Like the friend at our church, you may need time to heal. Or, like Lazarus, you may need others' help unwrapping you from what has bound you so long. But God promises the power of heaven behind your holy stand. He says to you, "Take your stand. Come out of death and into the life of favor I have planned for you. Your whole family, and the generations after you, can know your greatest season ever."

6

Unprecedented Upgrades

*The Importance of Raising Our Sights
to Honor God*

Sometimes the Lord wants to do a work in your life that I call an unprecedented upgrade. This is something you haven't experienced before in your walk with Jesus. It could be an unexpected blessing, a new season you enter into or a new sphere of influence you're given. It might be something you've longed for and dreamed about but never expected to happen. Then, finally, the season arrives when the Lord does it—and it amazes everyone.

God loves to bring about these unprecedented upgrades in our lives for two very simple reasons. First, it blesses us, and that delights Him. Second, it brings glory to His name, drawing the lost and suffering into His healing light.

I do a lot of traveling for ministry, and I take a lot of international flights. For some reason, I always end up in what I call seat 78B. It's a middle seat between two very large, burly men, and the flight is ten to twelve hours. I'm not an aggressive traveler, and I don't fight to command the elbow rests on either side of me. So, usually on those trips, I end up sitting with my knees pressed together and my elbows held in for a long, uncomfortable flight.

Things were a lot different for a woman who used to travel with our international ministry team. She constantly got upgrades. It started at the airline ticket counter, where out of the blue the representative would tell her, "Oh, look, we have an aisle seat left with a lot of leg room. Let me give that to you." Then when our team arrived at the hotel, the desk clerk would say to her, "Ah, I see there's a suite available. Let me give that to you for the same price."

She didn't have to be on ministry trips for this to happen. Friends and acquaintances called her whenever they were about to leave on vacation and said, "Our apartment in mid-town Manhattan will be empty for a week. Why don't you come and stay there while we're gone?" I once called her to see if she could meet with me on some matter. "Uh, I can't at the moment," she answered—because she was staying at some friends' house. In Switzerland. Only it wasn't a house. It was a castle!

I think my life is ready for some upgrades like hers. Don't you?

The rest of us were constantly awed at all the unbelievable upgrades that came her way, none of them solicited. I once asked her how this happened so often. She told me, "I actually pray for upgrades. I believe in my Abba Father's love, that He is a good Father and that He loves to give good gifts to all His children."

Some might say this is a covetous faith, but I say it's beautiful, simply because it comes from a beautiful view of the heavenly Father. Note that she said, "*All* His children." You see, she didn't just ask for upgrades for herself. She was always seeking them for others. In fact, she's the kind of person who thrills to see others blessed. This is what made her so effective as our ministry coordinator on international travels; she was always thinking of the people who were going to receive what we had to offer in ministry. When she saw how deeply the Lord blessed them, it constantly built up her view of the Father's giving, generous nature.

Too many of us see God the opposite way, as a judge who wields a threatening gavel, ready to bring it down on us in condemnation. Do you believe your Abba Father is always looking out for your best interests—not just for a good plane seat, but for your health, your marriage, your work and especially for those around you?

My friend's life demonstrates a great truth about our loving Father: It doesn't matter whether our issue is big or small. His loving favor toward us is the same all the time, because His giving nature never changes, no matter what our situation in life.

King Solomon's life illustrates powerfully how the Lord goes about providing unprecedented upgrades to His servants. In Solomon's day, Israel's countryside was dotted with places of worship known as high places. These were like minitemples, constructed as conveniences for God's people so they wouldn't have to travel all the way to Jerusalem to worship. But the Lord wanted His people in one place when they worshiped, so He considered those high places unworthy. In fact, the Lord ordered them all to be torn down.

Yet when King Solomon visited a town called Gibeon, he went to the local high place so he could worship God. Normally, this would have caused an outrageous scandal.

But Solomon's offering was full of sincere devotion and love for the Lord. He was so caught up in pure worship that he didn't bring the usual number of sheep to be sacrificed; he brought one thousand. God saw the intention in Solomon's heart and was delighted. He looked past the technicality of where the sacrifice took place, and He did something unprecedented: He told Solomon He would give him his heart's greatest desire.

It's a surprising story (see 2 Chronicles 1). Who would expect God to react to Solomon's actions this way? Yet there's a deep lesson in this for God's church today. It begins with the Lord's question to Solomon: "What is your heart's desire?"

What would you have asked for? I've thought of this question ever since I was a teenager, as my own faith was still being formed. In those youthful days, when life was still relatively simple, my desires all had to do with grand ambitions. Coming from a long line of ministers, I dreamed about evangelizing, ministering to others, seeing God's Kingdom work demonstrated on earth in dramatic ways.

Those are still my desires. But sadly, for most of us, life's humbling challenges have a way of causing us to lower our sights. Today, if I were to ask people in my church about their greatest desire, I wouldn't be surprised if they said, "Oh, Gary, just to be out of debt. I'd love a clean financial start." Or, "I really wish I had a more regular spiritual life. I think my devotional life falls short of what God wants for me." I would commend them for asking these things, because they are good things.

What do you think Solomon asked for? He answered the Lord, "I am young and do not know how to lead the people. The one thing I desire from You, Lord, is wisdom. I need Your guidance to know how to lead Your people well." In a word, Solomon's desire was about blessing others. And in the Lord's eyes, that already amounted to an upgrade. Yet God was so pleased with the king's response that He decided to upgrade him even further. The blessing He promised Solomon beyond this was unmatched wealth and fame.

Now, if you've been a Christian for any length of time, you've been taught not to covet material things. I couldn't blame you if you read this passage and wondered, "Hold it. Does God really bless people this way? That's such a worldly gift. Why would He indulge a man's flesh with this sort of blessing?"

Yet it was all part of God's greater plan for Solomon. Because of the king's wisdom and wealth, leaders from all over that region of the world would travel to meet him. And they would learn the secret of his blessed kingdom: that there was a gracious God behind it all.

That's right. Embedded in Solomon's story is a lesson on God's amazing grace and how He applies it. Think about how unlikely these upgrades were. After Solomon's sacrifice in the high place, God would have been right to say, "Sorry, Solomon, but you're worshiping in disobedience. I've instructed My people that I abhor the high places. I've made it clear they're not to worship there. I can't give you My favor because of the terrible choice you made."

Maybe you hear a similar voice in your head from time to time. It tells you, "You can't expect upgrades from God. Think of all your missteps. Your marriage isn't going to get better; it'll only get worse, because you keep failing. You have so many flaws that you'll never overcome them all. How can you expect anything from God?"

But Solomon's story tells us just the opposite about God's character. He is always there for us. It's never okay to sin, but when we do, His desire for us never changes. He still wants to make good things happen for us and through us. He is still our loving Father, and He is always looking to upgrade our life to one of abundance, to a life that's both blessed and blesses others.

**An important step in knowing the fullness
of God's favor involves something Paul speaks
about: the renewing of our minds.**

How do we transform our image of God from that of a punitive master who constantly holds a hammer over our heads to the image of a loving Father who honors our faith even when we fail Him?

We find a simple yet profound illustration in our own home life. If you're a parent, you don't want your kids to see you only as someone who disciplines them and never takes an interest in their desires. You hate the idea that they think of you as somebody ready to pounce on their mistakes instead of delighting in their dreams.

This doesn't mean kids don't need correction constantly! You're only being responsible when you teach them the proper way to do things, to learn to take correct steps, to act and behave in ways that are right. Yet while they're taking this instruction, they also have to know they're loved, that you're behind them and want them to thrive, and that you always have their best interests in mind.

That's our heavenly Father's heart toward His church. Correction should always be expected, but it isn't His core aim with us. It's just part of the experience of growing up in a loving household, and it's meant to lead us into the upgraded life He desires for us. None of His upgrades, however, are based on our performance. They come from the hand of our gracious God.

I learned how true this is through a trip Kelly and I took to Walt Disney World with our kids. We planned the trip way ahead of time and were looking forward to romping through the park with our kids. But just before the trip, Kelly broke her ankle and had to wear a cast. There was no way we were going to cancel the trip, so we decided I would wheel her through the amusement park in a wheelchair. We would have to settle for chasing our young ones as best we could.

That turned out to be idealistic. One of the first exhibits you see once you enter Magic Kingdom is a semicircle of stores on a crowded street. The area was packed—and I hate crowds, especially jostling, rude crowds on hot, humid days in the Florida summer. From the outset, it didn't look like the promising day we'd dreamed of. And it wasn't.

It took what seemed like forever just to move fifty feet or so through the crowd. In the rush to push through, people kept bumping into Kelly's chair. Already I was irritated, frustrated and cranky. I kept asking my wife, "Are you staying comfortable, honey?" But inside I was thinking, *This is so uncomfortable for me! Why didn't we do the smart thing and leave you in the hotel room? It's a mess trying to push you through these crowds.*

Finally, we came to the first ride the kids wanted us all to go on. We dutifully got in the line, which seemed to stretch forever. A few feet ahead of us was a sign providing an estimated wait time of 45 minutes. And we weren't in the shade.

Grumbling to myself, I noticed one of the park workers looking at us. He walked up to Kelly with a friendly smile and said, "Welcome. Listen, you don't have to wait in line. Since you're in a wheelchair, you and your family get to move to the front."

We did as he said—and suddenly the joy we'd wanted for our trip returned. The ride was great, so afterward we got in line again. And again. And again. There was no waiting for us at Disney that day, which in itself is a kid's dream come true. I didn't hesitate to let myself be that kid. What looked like one of the most miserable vacations of my life turned out to be one of the best we've ever had.

We all have wheelchairs in our lives, things we have to push around in a constant uphill chore: Kids in trouble. Tensions in marriage. Frustration at work. These things can overwhelm us. And yet sometimes in the midst of our misery, God taps us on the shoulder and says, "I have another line for you today. Come over here, into the shade, and go straight to the head of the line. This is much easier." God does this not because we've earned it. I certainly didn't that day. He does it to remind us that *He sees*. That He is there with us. And that our wheelchair doesn't define our lives; our relationship with Him does.

Sometimes we have to wait to receive the upgrade God has for us.

David had to endure an excruciating period before he received the upgrade God had for him. After King Saul's death, the kingdom of Israel was divided. David had authority over two tribes, while Saul's son, Ishbosheth, had power over ten. As a result, "There was a long war between the house of Saul and the house of David" (2 Samuel 3:1 ESV).

Years earlier, David had been anointed by the prophet Samuel to lead Israel. It was an unprecedented event, a farmer's son being called to rule as king. As a result, David knew his calling and destiny at an early age. Yet now, after all he had been through—deadly attacks from Saul, having to flee for his life, a divided kingdom—he must have wondered whether or not God's promise would ever come to pass.

But David didn't murmur or complain about what the Lord hadn't yet done in his life. Nor did he lose heart about the Lord's promise to him. He knew he was facing a long battle, perhaps with many losses to come. Yet he continued to believe God had his best interests in mind.

So how did David's unprecedented upgrade manifest? Scripture says, "David grew stronger and stronger, while the house of Saul became weaker and weaker" (v. 1 ESV).

Sometimes we can't imagine God transforming things for us—our tense marriage, our debt-ridden finances, our estranged relationships. Yet I can tell you unequivocally that God is at work making your household stronger and stronger. On the surface your situation may look worse, but He is cutting away at things with the sword of His Spirit, and He is putting into place building blocks of faith and trust. You can know the enemy's hold is getting weaker and weaker, while the work of the Spirit is making your household stronger and stronger.

Sometimes an unprecedented upgrade can be so out of the ordinary it's shocking—and it brings about overwhelming change. This kind of unprecedented upgrade is found in Numbers 27 in a story that doesn't get preached about much. Moses was presiding as judge over Israel when he was approached by the five daughters of a man who had just died. In the culture of that time, a family's inheritance went to the oldest son. But in this family, there was no son; there were only the five daughters.

The women were distraught because everything that their family had built up was about to be lost. They asked Moses, "Why should the name of our father be taken away from his

93

clan because he had no son? Give to us a possession among our father's brothers" (v. 4 ESV).

Moses knew this had never been done before, but he took the matter to the Lord. God's response amazed him: "The daughters of Zelophehad are right. You shall give them possessions of an inheritance among their father's brothers and transfer the inheritance of their father to them" (v. 7 ESV).

Here was a new decree—and it set a whole new precedent in Israel. From that time forward, any daughter who didn't have a brother could inherit the family's estate. The five daughters' request for an unprecedented upgrade didn't just change life for themselves; it opened the door for generations of others to be blessed.

Make no mistake about it: God wants your family to be blessed. He wants you to enjoy a happy marriage, blessed children and solid finances. But more importantly, God wants you to become a blessing. Like Solomon and the five bereaved daughters, the upgrades you receive may benefit many others.

What if those five daughters had settled for the status quo? They could have reasoned, "Things have always been this way. Who are we to expect such things from God? We aren't better than our forebears." Yet if they hadn't asked, generations would have missed out on a blessing God meant for many.

Does this describe you? Have you asked lately, "Lord, would You rekindle my marriage? Would You provide work for me that covers all my bills? Would You show me the ministry You want me to have for Your kingdom?" Maybe you think you're unworthy to ask for those things. Well, of course you're unworthy! Solomon was unworthy—but God honored his faith. Our Father delights to bless us with amazing upgrades for His name's sake.

Maybe you wonder why some people constantly get unprecedented upgrades while others don't. I think back to the woman on our international ministry team and all the amazing upgrades she received. I realize there was very little difference between her and the rest of us on the team. A lot of what she experienced had to do with her view of the Father. And a lot of what the rest of us experienced had to do with the inner voices we're prone to listen to that aren't His.

The story in the Bible that best illustrates this for me involves the twelve spies of Israel who went into Canaan to scout the land God had promised them (see Numbers 13). What they saw there was amazing. Talk about upgrades. The water in Canaan sparkled brighter, the fruit that hung from the trees was massive and the fields were infinitely greener. Yet when those spies returned, they were divided over their report. Ten of them said, "The land is indeed flowing with milk and honey. But it's also full of giants. They'll overwhelm us. There is no way the Lord is going to give us this land."

You probably know many Christians with this sort of attitude. Their view of life is, "Why should I be so selfish as to ask God for anything? He isn't likely to do that." No, the opposite is true. It would be *exactly* like God to do it for you!

The remaining two spies, Caleb and Joshua, knew this about the Lord's character. They said, "We, too, saw the land. And we saw the giants. Praise God, we know He wants to give us that land!"

Maybe, like Israel, you're sitting just outside the place God has intended for you. What's your attitude about it? Do you believe a life filled with God's purpose is too much to ask? Or do you believe that no weapon formed against you can prosper, that no giant is too big for your God to deal with?

Scripture says the ten doubting spies spread discouragement through Israel. In the end, those ten never entered Canaan. But Joshua and Caleb did. Tragically, if we continue in despair, it can become a self-fulfilling prophecy.

If you want to lead an upgraded life, I believe your steps will be marked by three things:

- *You'll constantly say, "Sign me up!"* Engage in the promises you see God give in His Word and say yes to all of them.
- *You'll ask boldly.* Be like the five daughters who approached Moses. Don't be ashamed or fearful to ask God to do what has never been done before, and expect to see His goodness in your life—and others'.
- *Believe that God delights to do it—because He delights in you.* It isn't prideful to ask Him for good things. Like those five daughters, you're looking to pass on the blessings of the family name, and there's no higher name than Christ's.

The upgraded life is one of unspeakable joy, and God wants to bless you with it. That's just one dimension of the amazing favor He has for you.

7

Overwhelming Victory

God's Desire to Supply You with All You Need

Hopefully you're starting to recognize the upgrades God has given you over your lifetime. As you tally them up, you can see a pattern of His faithfulness to you. You're encouraged—and the faith He restores in you makes you raise your sights in expectation to see more of His goodness.

I want to encourage you in that expectant hope, especially as the challenges of life continue to come. That's an important thing to remind you of as you start to enjoy God's upgrades: Life's challenges never stop coming. I'm always careful to caution Christians about this, especially in times of blessing.

Maybe you've heard the joke about the guy who unwittingly drove the wrong way on the freeway. His mistake wreaked havoc, making drivers do wild things to avoid hitting him. His wife saw a news flash about what was happening, and she decided to call her husband to warn him.

"Be careful. There's an idiot on the road," she said. "I can't talk now," her husband answered. "There are thousands of idiots on the road."

Sometimes the driver who sees multiple vehicles flying at him is the one doing the bad driving. We take a wrong turn on a freeway ramp, and suddenly trials careen at us with breakneck speed. It takes every ounce of our energy just to avoid disaster. I'm talking about crises anybody might face: mounting bills, broken relationships, job loss, alienated relatives. All of these crises challenge our faith, and when they mount too high for us to handle, our trust in God's wonderful favor can take an unwanted detour.

Sometimes doubts build up in us because we know life wasn't always this challenging. We may have enjoyed a long season of life when God's hand was clearly on us. Our prayers were answered with merciful grace, and we saw His goodness at work everywhere. Then suddenly everything was thrown into upheaval. Stuff came at us like speeding cars, and we jerked the steering wheel back and forth just to avoid crashing. Now life has continued that way for an extended time—and doubts about God's care have taken root. So we've started to question the reality of His promises.

I have a name for this season in life. I call it the Friday–Saturday Setback. I'm referring to the two days before Jesus' resurrection. For God's people, that Friday and Saturday seemed like the darkest stretch of their lives—and maybe all of history. Everything up to that moment had pointed to the fulfillment of God's kingdom on earth. In three years' time, Jesus performed miracles of healing and provision, showing compassion to people and giving them hope. He even resurrected a man who'd been dead for three days. For anyone in Israel who loved God, things could not have looked more promising.

Jesus' disciples had a front-row seat for it all. They even took part in the miracles He performed, feeding thousands with just a few bread loaves and fish. Those twelve men were the Master's closest friends and followers, and they had given up their lives to walk with Him. It was a mountaintop period for anyone who wanted his life to count for God.

Then came the Friday after Passover, and Jesus was arrested in the Garden of Gethsemane. From there, things happened so fast the disciples couldn't catch their breath. They saw Jesus beaten, maligned, spat upon and scourged. They saw Him led to court on trumped-up charges and judged by evil men.

I'm sure the disciples prayed the whole time that God would step in and deliver Jesus. But it didn't happen. To their horror, they watched as their Master was crucified, suffering a torturous death alongside convicted criminals. They saw His lifeless body carted away and sealed inside a tomb. End of story.

What began as a life with eternal promise—one meant to fulfill God's Word—couldn't have ended more dismally. It was a setback the disciples couldn't recover from.

Think about what that Friday and Saturday must have been like for the disciples. Those two days were filled with fear and confusion as the terrifying events came nonstop. The disciples were stunned by it all. A familiar scene from Luke 24 sums up their state of mind.

> That same day two of Jesus' followers were walking to the village of Emmaus, seven miles from Jerusalem. As they walked along they were talking about everything that had

happened. As they talked and discussed these things, Jesus himself suddenly came and began walking with them. But God kept them from recognizing him.

He asked them, "What are you discussing so intently as you walk along?"

They stopped short, sadness written across their faces. Then one of them, Cleopas, replied, "You must be the only person in Jerusalem who hasn't heard about all the things that have happened there the last few days."

"What things?" Jesus asked.

"The things that happened to Jesus, the man from Nazareth," they said. "He was a prophet who did powerful miracles, and he was a mighty teacher in the eyes of God and all the people. But our leading priests and other religious leaders handed him over to be condemned to death, and they crucified him. We had hoped he was the Messiah who had come to rescue Israel."

vv. 13–21

You can sense the despair dripping from their words. One phrase leaps out—"We had hoped" (v. 21)—revealing their hope was past tense. It was dawning on them that their dreams wouldn't come to pass after all. Unbelief crept in.

I know a lot of Christians who can identify with this. They wondered if God would ever answer their prayers, but things always seemed to get worse instead of better. Now, as they confront more oncoming trials, their hope in God's promises falls by the wayside. Like the men on the road to Emmaus, they tell themselves, "At one time, Jesus worked miracles in my life. But now He seems absent completely. I don't see any reality of God. Why should I keep believing?"

It's crucial not to make negative or disbelieving decisions during our Friday–Saturday Setback.

There's an instructive story in 2 Kings 5 about a man named Naaman. He was a great warrior, a top general in an army that was at war with Israel. But Naaman suffered from leprosy, and his condition was worsening. One of the servants tending to Naaman was a captured Israelite woman. Even though she knew him as an enemy soldier, she was heartbroken to see Naaman approaching death. She remembered the miracles God worked in Israel through the prophet Elisha, so she told Naaman and his family, "There's a prophet in Israel who can help you."

This was great news to Naaman's ears—and hearing it brought a surge of hope to his spirit. He had been convinced he was as good as dead, but now he had a chance. He got excited as he thought about being restored to life. Also encouraged was the king he served. With hope for his top general, the monarch instructed Naaman to go to Elisha, loading his entourage with 750 pounds of silver, 150 pounds of gold, and 10 sets of clothes to serve as a gift to the prophet. It was offered in gratitude for any healing Elisha could provide.

Naaman's spirits surely soared at this gesture. He must have thought, *God seemed to speak through the young maid. That gave me hope. And now I have the king's backing with these gifts of wealth. It all seems like a confirmation of something good to come. Certainly, Elisha will heal me. My life will be given back to me.*

When Naaman arrived and met Elisha, this indeed seemed to be the case. The prophet told the general that, yes, he would be healed. But first he instructed Naaman to go to the Jordan River and dip himself in the water seven times.

I can picture Naaman being a bit puzzled by this. If Elisha could heal him, why didn't he just wave his hand and pronounce him restored? Besides, the Jordan River looked sort of dirty, like it was the last place someone would find healing. How could those swirling brown waters cleanse anyone of leprosy?

Yet Naaman did as he was instructed. He went down to the river and dipped his leprous body into the water. Nothing happened. So he dipped again, and then a third time. No result. Now Naaman must have started to doubt. Why was this not working? If the water was going to heal him, why would it have to take four more times? He dipped again—a fourth time, then a fifth. Then he held up his arms to examine them. Nothing. Not even the tiniest change.

I wonder whether Naaman began to feel a dread in his gut. He had only two more chances to be healed, and so far there was no sign of change. Not even a glimmer. He might have wondered why he had gotten his hopes up in the first place. He probably thought that was worse than if he had simply made peace with death.

He drew a breath and dipped for the sixth time. Nothing.

Here is where I imagine every crushing doubt rushing into Naaman's mind like a flood. First, the empty promise of the maid. Then the foolish, blind belief of the king. Now the deception of the prophet. Naaman's heart might have turned completely dark at the cruelty of it all.

Instead, he dipped a seventh time. And the Bible says that as he emerged from the water Naaman's skin was like a baby's. None of the deadly leprosy remained. Instead, Naaman had a brand new, healthy body.

Despite every outward sign he wouldn't be healed, Naaman's hope never died. I believe God wants to speak this same hope into us. No matter what our trial—standing in hope for our children, for our finances, for our unsaved loved ones—He stands alongside us, sustaining us with the hope of a gospel that heals completely.

Paul poses a crucial question to anyone whose faith diminishes through their trials. Once again, I refer you to the great, faith-sustaining truth found in Romans 8:28: "We know that God causes everything to work together for the good of those who love God and are called according to his purpose for them." This amazing truth has brought hope to tens of millions. Yet the context of this passage is even more amazing.

Paul had just been writing about life in the Spirit. He says the Spirit-life we have in Christ determines how we view every event that we experience. No matter how many trials come at us, we can know God is at work shaping every part of them for our good. Then Paul adds this amazing statement: "If God is for us, who can ever be against us? Since he did not spare even his own Son but gave him up for us all, won't he also give us everything else?" (vv. 31–32).

In this amazing chapter, Paul is building for us a bedrock truth he wants every Christian to know: "Can't you see how easy it is for God to give you everything you need? He already gave you the hardest thing of all: His own Son, to die on the cross. Why would He withhold anything less?"

What a powerful truth. God held back nothing to provide our freedom from all bondage, including His precious Son. Now the same power that raised Jesus from the dead resides in us, raising us to newness of life. God is saying, "I didn't hold My Son back from you. And I won't withhold the power you need to overcome your crisis."

Still, many of us have trouble grasping this. We can be tempted to think God blesses only a certain type of Christian, mainly those whose faith seems greater than ours. We don't realize this belief makes us more vulnerable to Satan's accusations: "You aren't doing something right. Your walk isn't good enough. Why else would this be happening to you, and not to others?"

Such lies are meant to color our view of God's goodness and grace. And they're followed by other lies: "Nothing good is ever going to happen to you again. Why did you ever think you'd have God's favor? That was just a false promise you made to yourself. You've been a Christian long enough to realize you deserve what you're getting."

Paul steps in to give us weapons against these accusations. He provides a list of the amazing things our merciful Father does for us. Note how many times the phrase "for us" appears in this passage:

> Who dares accuse us whom God has chosen for his own? No one—for God himself has given us right standing with himself. Who then will condemn us? No one—for Christ Jesus died *for us* and was raised to life *for us*, and he is sitting in the place of honor at God's right hand, pleading *for us*.
>
> vv. 33–34, emphasis added

Finally, Paul offers assuring words to everyone who suffers:

> Can anything ever separate us from Christ's love? Does it mean he no longer loves us if we have trouble or calamity, or are persecuted, or hungry, or destitute, or in danger, or threatened with death? (As the Scriptures say, "For your sake we are killed every day; we are being slaughtered like sheep.") No, despite all these things, *overwhelming victory* is ours through Christ, who loved us.
>
> vv. 35–37, emphasis added

Overwhelming victory in the midst of our crises—what a gift for us! **Christ's overwhelming victory dwells in everyone who's convinced of His love despite their suffering.**

> I am *convinced* that nothing can ever separate us from God's love. Neither death nor life, neither angels nor demons, neither our fears for today nor our worries about tomorrow—not even the powers of hell can separate us from God's love.
>
> v. 38, emphasis added

In this powerful passage, Paul supplies us with a helpful word to cling to: *convinced*. It's the key to being freed from every doubt that comes with a Friday–Saturday Setback.

Amazingly, the conversation between the men going to Emmaus happened *after* the resurrection. Even Jesus' triumph over death wasn't enough to bring them back fully from doubt. They admitted,

> This all happened three days ago. Then some women from our group of his followers were at his tomb early this morning, and they came back with an amazing report. They said his body was missing, and they had seen angels who told them Jesus is alive!
>
> Luke 24:21–23

The men must have sounded doubtful about His resurrection, because Jesus rebuked them: "You foolish people! You find it so hard to believe all that the prophets wrote in the Scriptures. Wasn't it clearly predicted that the Messiah would have to suffer all these things before entering his glory?" (vv. 25–26). The message is clear: We can't let our Friday–Saturday Setback determine our belief in God's goodness.

105

Yet even when we have lingering doubts, God's grace flows freely to heal us. This happened for the disciple Thomas, who doubted the reports of his closest friends when they told him Jesus was alive. Thomas represents where a lot of devoted believers are today. I'm talking about those who once believed with zeal, who sacrificed to take part in Christ's glorious work and who rejoiced as they saw God visibly on the move, transforming lives. But then came a Friday–Saturday Setback, a lingering trial that dragged on for years. They never stopped going to church and hearing sermons about God's goodness. But something inside them died, and now they can't resurrect it. The lingering disappointment of their long, dismal setback has beaten them down too far.

Is this you? Jesus wants to come to you just as He did to Thomas. He wants to show you His scars from the worst possible Friday–Saturday Setback. He wants the power of His resurrection to raise you to life in a way you could never do for yourself. He wants to convince you of His eternal Word, to demonstrate through His resurrection that no lie or power can ever derail you from His kingdom purpose: "No power in the sky above or in the earth below—indeed, nothing in all creation will ever be able to separate us from the love of God that is revealed in Christ Jesus our Lord" (Romans 8:39).

Because of Jesus' loving grace, Thomas believed again. History tells us he became one of the most impactful of all the disciples. He took the gospel to India, where he founded influential churches in seven major cities. Today India has more Christians than any other nation in the world.

God won't withhold anything from us when it comes to our belief in Him. Jesus withheld nothing from Thomas when His friend needed to believe again. Jesus also calls you His friend, and He has withheld nothing to keep you in His loving favor.

> I no longer call you slaves, because a master doesn't confide in his slaves. Now you are my friends, since I have told you everything the Father told me.
>
> John 15:15

Let Jesus convince you again. He brings resurrection life to you in the midst of your trial. Like Thomas, you'll taste the glory of His favor again—and it will transform you. His overwhelming victory is one more dimension of His amazing favor to you.

PART III

OUR CALLING

Offering His Favor

8

Showing the Favor of God

A Favor Not Meant to End with Us

We've talked about what it means to find God's favor. It's one of the great privileges we have as Christians—to live under the blessed favor of the Creator of all things. Our Father opens a window from heaven and pours out on us His abundant, plentiful resources. Think about all the amazing things He supplies us with, sufficient for every area of life: forgiveness, acceptance, grace, blessings and power over the enemy. And He does all this because He loves us so much. Because of God's favor, His people can be a happy people on the earth. All of that is God's part in the process.

We've also talked about our part in the process of living in His favor—including the discipline needed to conquer our cynicism, the importance of taking a stand to change our family's destiny, the practice of raising our sights to trust in God's abilities, and knowing that He desires to give us all we need.

All these things are given to us for a great kingdom purpose. You see, there's another great privilege offered to us, one that's equal to living in God's favor. And that is showing the favor of God to others. We aren't meant just to receive His favor and stop there. We're to take what God has given us and, in joyful gratitude, share it with someone else.

What I'm talking about is a wholistic lifestyle of showing God's favor. It's a life marked by looking for opportunities to demonstrate His amazing favor to others—in our marriage, with our children, with our brothers and sisters in Christ and to the world around us. That's His plan behind all the blessings He gives us. We're to share them with the world to bring Him glory.

What does it look like, exactly, to show God's favor? To show favor is to demonstrate heaven in awesome acts of love. Love that changes lives. Love displayed in ways large or small. You may ask, But doesn't God demonstrate heaven through His presence in prayer meetings? Of course He does. When someone stands and gives a prophecy? Absolutely, yes. When a powerful sermon convicts the heart? No question. When we stand together in unified worship? Without a doubt.

Yet when we take His lavish love into the world around us—to our job, our school, our neighbor's house, even our own family—we demonstrate heaven's power at work on earth.

I love repeating a story that my father liked to tell on himself. To me, it shows how a Christian can move from the immense joy of finding God's favor to the even deeper joy of showing His favor to others.

My parents were on vacation in Florida while my dad was taking a brief sabbatical from pastoring at Times Square Church. He'd been a pastor for a few years, and the role kept him so busy that he felt a growing need to take time off to spend in God's presence. So, while my mom spent time shopping or lying on the beach, Dad spent his time in their hotel room praying. He was hungry for intimacy with God, so he spent four, five, six hours a day solely in prayer.

It was a great, refreshing time for him. He felt his burdens lifting and the joy returning to his heart. He benefited so deeply from those times of prayer that he began to think, "I can't believe the difference in my soul. Could this be what Moses experienced when he was on the mountain with God? Is it possible for the Lord's glory to settle on a person the way it did with Moses? When he came down from the mountain, the people were barely able to look at him because of the powerful glow of God's glory." The Bible has a word for that visible glow of glory. It's *shekinah*.

Dad wondered, "Does the Lord's shekinah glory actually shine forth from us if we spend enough time in His presence?"

One evening my parents dined out after another of my dad's marathon days of prayer. As he and Mom told each other about their day, they noticed that a certain server kept walking by their table. Each time she passed by, she took a long look at my father's face.

"See, I knew it!" Dad whispered to Mom. "She's seeing the shekinah glory on me."

The next time the server came by, she realized my parents noticed her long gazes. So she finally summoned the courage to walk over. "I'm sorry. I know I'm not your waitress, but I have to ask you something," she said. Then she leaned over the table, took a final long look at Dad and said, "Are you Hugh Hefner?" (If you don't know who Hugh Hefner was, I'd be proud to say I'm your pastor. Hefner was the founder of *Playboy* magazine.)

That was always the punchline to my dad's story. But I've taken the liberty to add a second part to the story. When we lived in Texas during my growing-up years, my mom and dad took us on a family vacation one summer to the mountains of Colorado. We stopped to have lunch at a diner somewhere along the way, and my dad got into a conversation with our server. She looked to be about college age. When Dad found out she was a Christian, he asked what she planned to do with her life. She answered that she'd just been accepted to college and was working to save up money for the fall semester. "I'm going to a school in Missouri," she said. "It's called Central Bible College. Have you heard of it?"

Heard of it? My dad had attended there! (It was also where I would go to college a few years later.)

I'd never seen my father do this before, but when the server disappeared to bring our dessert, he took a paper napkin and wrote this message on it: "I want to pay the tuition for your first two years of college. Here is my secretary's number. Call her, then read her this message on the napkin. She'll arrange it all for you."

When the server returned, my dad pushed the napkin across the table to her. She picked it up curiously, and we all watched as her eyes darted from line to line on the note. Finally, she buried her face in her hands and burst into tears. She was so happy!

I'm convinced the expression we all saw on that young server's face was God's shekinah glory. My father demonstrated God's favor—a favor he himself had known—and it found its ultimate purpose in another person's life.

That kind of gesture would be a huge sacrifice for most of us. But even a small gesture can demonstrate God's glory when we show His favor to others. I believe my dad was tuned in completely to the Holy Spirit when he offered that gift to the young woman. It didn't change the world, but it changed *her* world.

You never know when God wants to use you to do something small but magnificent—something that changes the path of another person's life forever.

Second Kings 6–7 contains one of the most powerful examples of what it means to show God's favor. Jerusalem was surrounded by the vast army of an enemy king, Ben-Hadad. The enemy encamped around the city, cutting off all supplies to the starving Israelites. As the people grew weak from hunger, they all looked to Elisha, the prophet, for a word from the Lord. But the message he gave them wasn't encouraging. He told the people, "This siege is going to continue. Food will be scarce, and it will become so costly no one will be able to afford it."

An assistant to Israel's king grew angry when he heard this. He rejected Elisha's prophecy outright, saying, "That will never happen! This enemy won't surround us much longer. We'll have plenty of food soon." But Elisha answered, "No, you're about to see what happens. Eventually, God is going to act on our behalf, that's true. But you personally won't experience it." In other words, Israel would see the Lord demonstrate to them His favor, but the king's assistant wouldn't experience it for himself, because he didn't believe God's word initially.

While all this took place, four lepers sat far outside Jerusalem witnessing the siege. Their affliction prevented them from being inside the city walls, and like their fellow Israelites, they were starving. Finally, they reasoned, "If we stay here and do nothing, we'll die. Let's at least go to the enemy camp and beg for scraps. If they kill us, they kill us. But that's better than starving to death out here with no chance at all. Let's set out tomorrow and see what the Lord might do."

The next morning, they went to the enemy's camp—and they found it deserted! The Holy Spirit had supernaturally frightened all the soldiers and scattered them. In their hurry to escape, they left behind everything: food, wine, supplies, medicines, clothes, tents, even gold and silver. As the lepers stumbled onto these treasures, they couldn't believe their good fortune. They were miraculously saved!

Imagine the starving men's excitement as they feasted on the amazing food. What a miracle! They'd thought they were finished, gone, as good as dead—but now they were alive again. And they had a heavenly table of God's bounty spread before them.

As they filled their stomachs, they told each other, "We've got to make sure we keep this stuff safe for ourselves. We should hide it." But one of them answered, "No, what we're doing isn't right. How can we feast this way while our brothers and sisters sit starving in Jerusalem? This is a day of good news for all of God's people. If we stay silent, punishment will surely overtake us. We need to tell the king what God has done."

This leper demonstrated what we all need to know about God's favor: *Good news is meant to be shared.*

Nevertheless, Israel's king was suspicious when he heard the lepers' tale. The enemy had oppressed Jerusalem for so long it was hard for the king to believe God would move in such a way. So he sent a group of spies into the enemy camp to see if what the lepers said was true.

I think a lot of Christians today are like the king: They've lived for so long under a dark cloud that they tend to doubt when they hear something good the Lord has done. They're tempted to give in to cynicism, thinking, "I've learned to expect suffering in my life. It's best not to get my hopes up."

But, of course, the Israelite spies came back saying the lepers' story was true. The windows of heaven had indeed opened—and now everyone in the city had all the supplies they needed for themselves and their children, from food to clothes to medicine. Suddenly, the famished Israelites stampeded through the city gates to get food to eat. The king's assistant tried to stop them, but nothing was going to keep God's people from His glorious provision. The assistant ended up getting trampled to death.

I believe some people today experience a kind of spiritual death, like the king's assistant. We waste years living with a false perception of God, believing He purposely withholds His favor, that we're not worthy to receive it. We think persecution and oppression are exactly what we need and deserve. "It's for my own good," we reason.

Of course, it's important to acknowledge there are times of trial and difficulty in life. But there are also times when God chooses to bless us unexpectedly, and in those times we're to enjoy His blessings without reservation. Paul makes this clear when he says, "I know how to be brought low, and I know how to abound. In any and every circumstance, I have learned the secret of facing plenty and hunger, abundance and need" (Philippians 4:12 ESV).

Many Christians know how to be abased, but they don't know how to abound. They reject the thought that God can heal them when they're sick, that He can deliver them from an addiction, that He can make their marriage a joy instead of a constant hardship. But it's crucial to believe God can heal us—and, more importantly, that He desires to.

Paul promises us, "God will generously provide all you need" (2 Corinthians 9:8). Note the word *all* here. That's what the starving people of Jerusalem experienced: *All* of their needs were supplied by God in an instant. In fact, they got more than they needed with the enemy army's treasure trove.

God's powerful promise of generosity is meant for every believer, in every generation. Yet Paul adds a statement that increases the verse's importance: "God will generously provide all you need. *Then* you will always have everything you need and *plenty left over to share with others*" (v. 8, emphasis added).

If this isn't the same message as the lepers' story in 2 Kings 7, I don't know what is. God wants to supply all your needs—not some, but *all*—because that's His nature, to give generously. And as we His people are lavishly blessed by Him, we're meant to give generously to others.

Let me point out something very important about the context of this passage. When Paul wrote it to the Corinthians, he was explaining to them the needs of the Church in Jerusalem, which was enduring a famine and close to starvation. Yet the Corinthians themselves were in need also, teetering on the edge of poverty. Still, Paul urged them to give not based on their ability but on God's ability to take care of all their needs. He told them:

> Don't give reluctantly or in response to pressure. "For God loves a person who gives cheerfully." And God will generously provide all you need. Then you will always have everything you need and plenty left over to share with others. As the Scriptures say, "They share freely and give generously to the poor. Their good deeds will be remembered forever."
>
> 2 Corinthians 9:7–9

The Corinthians and other churches in the region gave as much as they could, despite their own need, to bring aid to their desperate brothers and sisters. It was a major way of showing God's favor.

If you think it might be risky or painful to show favor by giving, I want to assure you of this: Whatever you can offer reverberates powerfully. It doesn't matter how small an amount you may give, because God multiplies its impact by His power. Whenever we do this—when we give to the needy in His name—they remember it forever, as the verse says. Let me prove it to you.

If you show God's favor as His Spirit directs you,
you'll be blessed to see how far even
a small gesture can go.

Two decades ago, I was on staff as a pastor at Times Square Church when a young man came to my office. He had moved to New York a few years earlier wanting to be an actor. But things hadn't worked out, and he was hustling to make a living. Broke and homeless, he'd ended up dealing drugs. It wasn't what he'd hoped for when he brought his dreams to New York, and he was embittered by the experience.

I told him about God's love for him, but he stopped me in my tracks. "It's easy for you to talk about God's love," he said. "You're sitting in this nice office. And I'm sure you're paid well. You wear nice clothes. And I know those cowboy boots you're wearing are worth something."

I had lived in Texas, and I kept wearing boots to keep some of its culture in my life. But I could see the hurt in this young man. So I decided to do something my father had done years before, when he could barely afford to do it. "I tell you what," I said. "These boots look like they might fit great on you. Why don't you try them on?" As I slid the boots off my feet, he looked at me as if I were crazy. He was still slack-jawed as he tried them on—and, sure enough, they were a perfect fit. He still hadn't said a word when he stood up and gave me a big hug.

He left that day knowing that church people didn't just talk about God's love; they demonstrated it. I knew I could afford another pair of boots, but that wasn't the point. He couldn't afford even one pair.

Everywhere this young man walked after that he was reminded of God's love for him. I found that out two years later when I received a call from a pastor friend in North Carolina named Steve. "Gary, I don't think you're going to believe this," Steve said. "Do you remember giving away your cowboy boots to a homeless kid in New York?"

"Yeah, I think I do," I said, vaguely remembering.

"Well, he's been wandering around the country ever since, haunted by that one act of love, saying, 'Jesus loves me. He really loves me.' Right now he's sitting in my office with tears in his eyes, saying he wants to get right with God."

Steve later helped the young man enter a drug rehabilitation program. But before we hung up, he said, "Shoot, just giving somebody your boots? That's easy!" We marveled over how God's kingdom works—that the most powerful, eternal, profound outcomes happen through the simplest acts of love. Showing favor to one bitter person can mean the difference in eternity.

God's favor is never meant to end with us. Showing favor means taking hold of the precious resources we're given—grace, forgiveness, blessing, authority—and bringing them to another person, saying, "This would fit perfectly in your life." It's kind of like saying to a broken, dream-shattered homeless kid, "These fancy boots would look great on you. Try them on!"

I believe if the lepers had kept their treasure hidden, their joy would have been short-lived. And I can tell you with authority, if you want joy in your life, don't go around looking for it. Give your life away, and the joy of heaven will follow. What you give will come back to you in a moment when you never thought you'd need it. It's happened for me.

In the opening chapter I told you about the heavy time that my wife, Kelly, and I went through with the miscarriage of our second child. Nothing on earth can take away the pain of that kind of experience. But a friend of ours did something beautiful for us that raised our sights to Jesus. Melody Green, the widow and ministry partner of the late musician Keith Green, stepped in to pay for the funeral of our little one. All these years later, I've never forgotten what Melody did—and I never will. We didn't need the money she offered, but that isn't what stayed with us. What remains today is a loving gesture that said, "I stand with you in your deepest pain."

That's the sort of selfless, empathetic-showing favor I saw again and again as pastor of The Springs Church. During a sermon I once spoke about a single mom in need who attended our church. Her husband had abandoned her and her children. Immediately after the service I was approached by another single mom who was going through the exact same thing and had the same financial need. She took my hand and said, "I don't know who she is," nodding toward the woman I'd spoken about, "but could you give this to her?" I looked down to see a wad of cash pressed into my hand.

Others in our congregation caught on to the high calling— and yes, the deeper blessing—of showing God's favor. A building contractor heard that the first single mom was looking to further her education so she could find a better paying job to support her children, and he offered to pay half of her college needs. That same week, another businessman came forward saying he wanted to pay for half of the woman's education. Without knowing it, their combined efforts allowed the mom to go to school full-time. But God's favor for her didn't end there. A woman working in the same field that the mom wanted to study came to me with her own offer: "Pastor Gary, I'll take her into work with me until she goes to college. Then, when she's ready to enroll, I'll go with her to show her the classes she needs."

All of these givers testify to feeling more blessed than the ones who received their generosity. They feel something unique, and there's a reason for that. You see, when you show God's favor, you take on His very nature—one of joyful, delighted, continual generosity.

Do you want spiritual power in your life? Do you want your prayers to be answered? Then show God's favor at every opportunity. When you do, you take on His own nature, and there's no greater blessing than that.

9

Proclaiming Your Favor

Aligning Ourselves with God
to See Our Breakthrough

It doesn't matter how long you've walked with God. At every stage of life we face times when we need a breakthrough of some kind. We face strains in our relationships, whether they're with family or friends. We face ups and downs with finances. We face a changing culture and a changing world with events and upheavals that can be frightening.

Sometimes the issue is a health matter, when a loved one or even our own life hangs in the balance. When I started writing this chapter, a friend's wife in Texas was facing one more surgery in a long line of procedures meant to preserve her life. When I told my friend, "I'm praying for her," I wanted him to know I wasn't just offering timid words; I was laying hold of heaven for his wife. Just a few months before I had asked all my friends for prayer. I had to have my thyroid removed when a cancerous spot was found on it. So

I, too, know the emotional roller coaster of waiting to hear a doctor's words about what might lie ahead. (Thankfully, my surgery was a success, and my prognosis remains very, very good.)

All of these issues carry with them agonizing struggles that can bring us to a breaking point—meaning, the point where we need a breakthrough. When that point comes, there are two ways we can approach the Lord in our crisis. The first is through *petition*. This is our deep cry of the heart, a pleading for help, an utterance of desperate need. I've had many times in life when I was compelled to petition the Lord, crying as the psalmist did so often, "How long, O Lord, before you hear me and answer?"

King Hezekiah of Israel made that kind of petition before God in Isaiah 37. Once again, the Israelites found themselves surrounded by a massive enemy, as the Assyrians formed a threatening circle around Jerusalem. And just like the previous enemy, the Assyrians cut off all outside help from the city so God's people would eventually starve to death. Meanwhile, the Israelites who were caught outside Jerusalem's walls had scattered. Agonizing for his city, King Hezekiah could only pace back and forth with worry.

Yet this attack wasn't just targeted at their material goods; it was psychological. Assyria's king sent a letter to Hezekiah telling him, "Don't let your God, in whom you trust, deceive you with promises" (Isaiah 37:10). What an accusation. If you're a Christian, you know exactly where this message came from. As God's children, we know our Lord's promises are ironclad and absolutely true. Yet in our crisis, the enemy will always try to convince us we're deceived if we keep believing in God's goodness. **More than any other weapon, this is the one Satan uses against God's people.**

Sadly, we sometimes succumb to the devil's accusations. How many times have you heard the following lies and accepted them? "You're wasting your time praying." "You've asked a hundred times and never been answered." "You've failed too often for God to speak to you anymore." "It's too late for you. Nothing will ever change." "The Lord has given up on you."

I picture Hezekiah being tempted to give up. The Israelites' situation was so desperate that Assyria's accusation seemed true. But Hezekiah refused to give in. Instead, he laid the demonic letter before the Lord and petitioned Him in prayer:

> O Lord of Heaven's Armies, God of Israel, you . . . alone are God of all the kingdoms of the earth. You alone created the heavens and the earth. Bend down, O Lord, and listen . . . to Sennacherib's words of defiance against the living God. It is true, Lord, that the kings of Assyria have destroyed all these nations. And they have thrown the gods of these nations into the fire and burned them. But of course the Assyrians could destroy them! They were not gods at all—only idols of wood and stone shaped by human hands. Now, O Lord our God, rescue us from his power; then all the kingdoms of the earth will know that you alone, O Lord, are God.
>
> Isaiah 37:16–20

I get encouraged when I read Hezekiah's words here. I believe the Lord is absolutely thrilled when He sees a petitioning heart like the king's. It's a heart that says, "Lord, I've spent too many sleepless nights worrying and obsessing over what I can't control. Now I come to You in trusting faith. You're the true God who holds every solution to every dilemma. No problem is too hard for You, no enemy too strong, no wall too high. I know You hold my breakthrough."

There's a second way to approach the Lord for a break-through—a way that delights Him but, sadly, few Christians choose. I'm talking about proclamation. It goes a step far-ther than petition. A petition is basically a plea, a hope, a trust—but proclamation actually claims our breakthrough based on God's Word. It envisions His answer to our crisis and declares in faith, "Thus says the Lord . . ."

Do you see the difference? Petition asks the Lord to hear our cry. But proclamation declares God has already heard our cry and is at work creating our breakthrough. I wrote in an earlier chapter that in our darkest times God is never idle; He's always at work on our behalf, shaping how He'll show us His favor. Proclaiming His favor means believing this—and then getting up off our knees and moving forward in faith.

The book of Hebrews defines faith, according to the King James Version, as "the substance of things hoped for, the evi-dence of things not seen" (Hebrews 11:1). What a wondrous, beautiful description. You probably know people with this kind of faith. They're the ones who proclaim breakthroughs as easily as they breathe, based on their faith in God's good-ness. These people stir my faith to action. And that's exactly what a proclaiming faith does: It infuses the people around you with greater faith, empowering them to take greater ac-tion in Jesus' name.

The prophet Isaiah stepped into Hezekiah's crisis with a proclaiming faith. While the Assyrians threatened Jerusalem, King Hezekiah spent all his energy petitioning the Lord. In the meantime, Isaiah was busy proclaiming God's favor. He prophesied to the people how the Lord was going to protect Jerusalem: "'He will not enter this city,' says the LORD. 'For my own honor and for the sake of my servant David, I will defend this city and protect it'" (Isaiah 37:34–35). Isaiah knew the Lord was faithful—that God alone held Israel's solution—and he spelled it out for the people so they could see His goodness and be encouraged by it.

Friend, you don't have to be a prophet to proclaim God's favor. In basic terms, a proclaimer of God's favor focuses on the solution rather than the problem. This Christian knows God has already prepared His answer—and he declares it. I'm not speaking of a reckless, name-it-and-claim-it type of approach to faith that sees something it desires and says, "That's mine. I deserve it, so I claim it." Nothing about that sort of attitude reflects God's favor; all it reflects is a covetous heart. I'm talking about something utterly different. See if you know what I mean.

I don't know about you, but I love working with solution-focused people. For a pastor especially, it makes a huge difference in the life of a church. Once, after a fierce storm struck Colorado Springs, I dreaded walking into our church the next day. I was worried how severe the damage might be. But when I arrived I was surprised to see that the place looked as good as new.

Our operations leader walked up to me smiling. "Pastor Gary, the sanctuary was flooded last night and the lights blew out," he said. "But we called a company to come in, and they drained all the water while the electricity got fixed. Then we spent the night sweeping out the floors and cleaning up. Don't worry, we're good to go for the worship services this morning."

What a joy that was to hear! Nobody had to tell our operations leader what was needed. And he didn't sit around worrying about the problem. Instead, he envisioned what was needed and got to work on the solution.

Wouldn't it be nice if all of life were like that? How would you feel if your math-challenged child strode up and said,

"Don't worry, Mom. I know my grade is low, but I called a tutor, and I'm getting up to speed. Problem being solved."

I'm joking here, but God does seem to honor solution-seeking prayers. It's because this kind of praying Christian assumes God's goodness—and she longs with all her being to see the Lord enter her difficult situation. She has an attitude of the heart that says, "I know my God is greater than this problem. He can do all things, and through His power I can overcome this."

God delighted to answer Hezekiah's petition and Isaiah's proclamation, and He did it in dramatic fashion:

> That night the angel of the LORD went out to the Assyrian camp and killed 185,000 Assyrian soldiers. When the surviving Assyrians woke up the next morning, they found corpses everywhere. Then King Sennacherib of Assyria broke camp and returned to his own land. He went home to his capital of Nineveh and stayed there.
>
> Isaiah 37:36–37

The Lord came through on what He promised. And the people saw that their God held all their breakthroughs.

Proclamation happens when someone is willing to stand up in a terrible situation and say, "I believe God has a different story to tell." I've partnered in prayer with brothers and sisters who have this kind of proclaiming faith. Kelly and I know a wonderful woman named Becky whose son, Isaiah, was born with an unnatural trachea. A bone was missing, and Isaiah needed surgery to insert a feeding tube down his throat. If he survived the procedure, doctors said he'd have to live with the tube permanently.

Becky was shaken. She dreaded the thought of her son having that kind of life. But she's also a prayer warrior full of breakthrough-type faith. We immediately joined with her to petition the Lord about Isaiah, crying out our need for a miraculous healing. Then at some point we were stirred to go beyond petition, and we started proclaiming the healing we believed God held for Isaiah.

I'll never forget coming home to Kelly and seeing a brilliant look across my wife's face. "They operated on Isaiah's trachea today," she said. "Gary, they found a bone that wasn't there before. God healed Isaiah. He's going to be fine!"

The Lord had a different story to tell than the one the doctors told. He created a bone where there was none. That is the healing, answering, favoring God we serve.

> **Kelly and I ending up having to experience this for ourselves, believing God had a different story to tell about our child.**

I've never petitioned God harder in my life than I did over my son, Elliot, when he was heavily addicted to drugs. I wrote earlier about Kelly's and my praying for our sons in utter desperation. This was especially true during the long period when we didn't know where Elliot was. I'm almost embarrassed to admit the weepy prayers I made during that time, but any parent in my situation would surely understand my agony: "God, how long? How long will my son be addicted? How long will he be homeless? How long will he be lost out there? And how long will this pain, this agony, go on for my wife and me? Show us your mercy, Lord."

These prayers became a routine for me, night after night, week after week. Then one night I heard the Lord's Spirit speak to my heart very clearly. He said, "It's time to stop asking Me, Gary. It's time to wipe your tears and dry your eyes. From now on, I want you to raise your hands and say, 'Thank You, Jesus. My son is coming home.'"

I hadn't seen any evidence of what God was telling me. But I knew it was coming to pass, that the Lord was faithfully at work making it happen. No one had taught me this. I didn't learn it from a seminar or book. The only thing I was consulting at the time was the Scriptures. But I started giving thanks in advance for the homecoming I knew we were going to experience. I praised, "Thank You, Jesus, that Elliot is coming home. Thank You that You're working out his deliverance at this very moment. Thank You that even though he's still out there, he's being set free." After two months of tearful petitioning, my prayers became a courage-fueled proclamation.

Let me note something important here. I didn't move abruptly from petitioning to proclaiming. Part of God's hidden work during our petitioning period is the work He does on our heart. That means we have to give our petition time. Only the Lord knows when to move us on to proclamation, and His Spirit is faithful to stir us when that hour comes.

This exposes a problem I see in many prosperity churches. Often their messages encourage people to begin with proclamation. Yet that bypasses the work of the heart God performs in us while we're petitioning Him. Sometimes when a person moves straight to proclamation, his heart is never truly engaged with God. And that's contrary to what He wants for us. Jesus looks to bear our pain and our tears as well as our desires—yet some Christians never give Him that chance. That kind of approach can actually disrupt our sanctification, meaning the ongoing work of the Holy Spirit in our lives. He sanctifies us by engaging our whole person, never bypassing any part of us, including our sadness and grief.

Had Kelly and I not endured our dark night of the soul over our son, we never could have developed the empathy we have for other parents and children going through what we did. The Lord had a purpose in it all. And when our healing came, it was that much sweeter.

Isaiah came to Hezekiah in the midst of the king's gut-wrenching cries of pain. Isaiah told the king, "I have another word for you, Hezekiah. Something different is happening now. The Lord wants you to know your crops are going to be plenteous. Your fields will be full. Your harvest will come in like never before. And all your people who have scattered will come back to Jerusalem."

Hezekiah must have done a double take. What could Isaiah mean? They were surrounded by thousands of Assyrians!

The prophet explained, "The king of Assyria will not come near this city. Not one arrow will even be shot toward these walls." It was a bold assertion—and Isaiah delivered it with authority.

I don't know about you, but when I hear a report like that one, delivered with the authority of heaven behind it, it stirs my faith. It's contagious! And that's exactly what happened with King Hezekiah. He believed. And God rescued His people in a way they never could have foreseen.

When we proclaim God's favor, we display to the world an important side of His incredible nature.

Proclaiming God's favor is part of our faithful service to Him. In fact, when Jesus taught us to pray, He included proclamation. It's all contained in the Lord's Prayer. According to Jesus, here is petition: "Give us today the food

131

we need . . . Don't let us yield to temptation, but rescue us from the evil one" (Matthew 6:11, 13). That declares our need. Then, here is proclamation: "May your will be done on earth, as it is in heaven" (v. 10). This declares what our Father wants to do, and it proclaims that He already holds our answer and desires to make it happen.

Jesus clearly affirms both petition and proclamation. There's certainly a time to pray, "Lord, if it's Your will . . ." There comes a time, however, when we're to remind ourselves, "Thus says the Lord . . ." You see, praying His will aligns our spirit with His, and that builds in us a holy confidence. Now as we pray we're not just voicing our own desire, but we're speaking from a heart that's infused with His truth. Praying His will isn't just about claiming something for ourselves; it's about declaring who God is! And proclamation doesn't end with declaring His will. Jesus gives us all authority to see our breakthrough manifested: "Look, I have given you authority over all the power of the enemy, and you can walk among snakes and scorpions and crush them" (Luke 10:19).

The apostle Peter was present when Jesus gave the disciples this promise of kingdom authority. That promise came flooding back to Peter one day after the resurrection, as he and John walked to the Temple. They came across a man who couldn't walk and was begging. Peter had seen Jesus demonstrate kingdom authority again and again. Now the apostle knew what was being required of him: to proclaim God's favor to this man. "What I do have I give to you," Peter said, indicating the authority he'd been given. "In the name of Jesus Christ of Nazareth, rise up and walk" (Acts 3:6 ESV). The man was instantly healed.

That miracle turned the Temple crowd upside down. It completely transformed their understanding of the God they worshiped—and showed them that His kingdom was in their midst.

If we're still petitioning when we should be proclaiming, we cast aspersions on God's character.

Most of us are tempted to keep petitioning when it's clearly time to proclaim. When we do this, we're saying, "Lord, I know You have my solution. But I don't know if You'll follow through with it." In essence, we refuse to join God's work in faith; instead, we ask Him to do everything. It all comes from a heart of unbelief.

Do you struggle to keep up hope for a wayward child? For your troubled marriage? For an addictive habit you can't break? God may be moving you out of petition and into proclaiming your victory. That may require you to proclaim, "My marriage is coming together." "My children are serving the Lord." "I'm walking in freedom from addiction to nicotine." Our Savior has the power to raise the dead, and He wants to resurrect your crisis into abundant life.

It won't matter if anyone around you agrees with your proclamation. What matters is that He does. When you proclaim it, you echo what He has already said about your situation. You may not see your answer yet, but He has formed it in eternity. And He is pleased by your proclamation of favor. Expect to see your loving Father answer you.

PART IV

A HIGHER CALLING

God's Over-the-Top Favor

10

Special Favor

Hearing the Call to a Higher Love

Everyone wants to be special. The world knows this, and tons of businesses capitalize on it. You see the evidence every day in your inbox, in your mailbox, on your device screen: offers for different levels of "specialness," just for doing business with this or that company. Hotels, airlines, clothing stores, even coffee shops, dangle gold, silver and bronze levels for their participating members. The more you patronize their service, the higher you get bumped up in membership, with all kinds of rewards and discounts. They make you feel a special kind of favor for choosing their business.

Yet there's another kind of special favor we can receive, a different kind of favor, that comes on a more personal level. This is the special favor shown by friends who go the extra mile for us. I needed this type of favor a few years ago when I broke my back in a car accident and was going to be incapacitated for a long while. Suddenly, my family and I were in great need of help.

That's when a young couple who works with our ministry stepped in. They had only been married a short while, but they chose to go so far as to move into our home to help make our lives easier. They had jobs of their own to go to, yet they spent their free time going to the grocery store for us, cooking for us, cleaning for us and doing every kind of chore a family needs. Household things seem minor when you can do them yourself, but they loom large when you can't. Doing those things for us helped our family get through an extremely hard season.

I still shake my head in wonder at the sacrifice that young couple made. Can you imagine the kind of love it takes to do that for a friend? They blessed us with a devotion I'll never forget. Kelly and I will always hold them in a special place in our hearts. What they showed us truly was special favor.

Yet God shows His people a type of favor that's even more special than this.

Paul introduced the Philippians to the concept of God's special favor.

I am certain that God, who began the good work within you, will continue his work until it is finally finished on the day when Christ Jesus returns. So it is right that I should feel as I do about all of you, for you have a special place in my heart. *You share with me the special favor of God.*

Philippians 1:6–7, emphasis added

Paul is telling the Christians in Philippi, "You and I have something in common as followers of Jesus. We belong to a special, unique kind of group. It's a group where God shows us His special favor."

Anyone reading this passage would think, *Sign me up! That sounds like God's gold package. And I want the best of everything that the Lord has for me. If knowing His favor is as awesome as I've known so far, how much greater is it to know His* special *favor?*

Yet, as you might guess, God's favor is a lot different from the world's. Paul points this out, completing the last verse: "You share with me the special favor of God, both in my imprisonment and in defending and confirming the truth of the Good News" (v. 7). Wait, what? Is Paul saying he was shown God's special favor by being *sent to jail*? How could being shackled and silenced reveal favor? This great apostle had preached to thousands, seeing crowds fall to their knees crying out for salvation. He appeared before kings, judges, governors, philosophers and other prominent people of his day. He received great spiritual revelations from the Lord, including a personal revelation of Jesus Himself. That's what favor sounds like to me. How does descending from all that into a prison cell become *special* favor?

Contrary to all reason, Paul describes his dark situation as if it were a gold-level club membership. And he thanked the Philippians for supporting him in his imprisonment, just the way I was thankful for the young couple who chose to support me. You see, what Paul describes here has to be translated through a spiritual heart. He's showing us that God is likely to bring us into unlikely places when He wants to accomplish a special kingdom work in our lives. **Paul knew that God's favor isn't only on us when things are going great.**

The opposite can be true, in fact. Sometimes it's when life becomes hardest that God shows us His greatest favor.

I have a friend who was on the worship team of a church I once pastored. When a young woman began attending, my friend was smitten with her. She'd only been a Christian for a short while and had a rough background. But my friend fell in love with her, and they ended up marrying. The dreams he'd held for so long in his walk with Jesus were coming to pass. Time after time he told me, "Gary, I'm so blessed to be with her. The favor of God is all over me."

But their marriage took a downturn. The wife reverted to her old lifestyle, falling deeper into an addiction until finally she left my friend for good. He was devastated, inconsolable—over not only the wife he lost but also a sense of losing God's presence. "I thought I was following His leading when we married," he told me. "I don't know what to think now."

As my friend walked through that trial, he could have turned to a certain teaching that many hurting Christians cling to. It states, "Don't worry; everything will be fine. God is going to work it all out for you."

I have to admit, it angers me to hear this type of message preached, because it does Christians a horrible disservice. People's hurts are real. And when their trials get worse instead of better, they're left scratching their heads. Then when things take a final tragic turn, they're devastated even more. Now they have nowhere to go with their broken heart, since God was supposed to make everything fine. It's no wonder so many wounded people limp away from the church for good.

As a pastor, I have some hard news for you: Not everything turns out fine. Not all marriages last. Not all people recover from their addictions. I've buried some people in our church that I shouldn't have had to, including young people. There are many reasons why tragedies take place.

My point is this: The world we live in and the trials we face are real. And we need a very real, faithful God who will walk lovingly beside us as we go through those trials. In fact, we need His special favor to get us through them.

Is there a crisis in your family? Is it financial? Relational? Circumstantial? Emotional? Jesus wants you to know He's with you—that He has His hand on your shoulder, His arms around you and His strength underneath you to carry you through your dark hour.

When my friend's wife returned to a sinful lifestyle, she made a choice. That choice wasn't God's choice for her; it was her own. And it wounded her husband and destroyed her marriage. My friend could have become bitter. So many Christians do when they experience losses like his. They think they've lost any favor they ever had. But that isn't God's way of doing things. He's not a God who looks to take away good things from us; He looks for ways to *bless us*. He is out for our good, even to restore what has been taken away.

Despite his crippling pain, my friend held on to his faith. He battled through that excruciating trial, and God kept building his strength. His circumstances didn't change, but everyone who knew him sensed his heart was gradually moving from bronze to silver to gold in God's kingdom. The Lord had more in store for his life, and it would only come through his special favor.

If ever a child of God might be convinced he lost the Lord's favor, it was David. If there was one Israelite who obviously knew God's favor, it was the amazing young man anointed to be Israel's king. From a young age David had everything going for him. He was a mighty warrior whom King Saul wanted by his side in battle. David was handsome and talented, a musician who wrote songs that God's people still sing today. And he was charismatic. When Saul's armies returned in victory, the crowds cheered for David more than they did the king. Everything he touched seemed blessed by God's favor.

But something went wrong in David's life. In fact, everything did. David's brothers were jealous of him. So was Saul, who flew into sudden rages and tried to kill David on several occasions. Finally, David had to flee, hiding in a cave in the wilderness. All that authority and respect he had enjoyed—talk about knowing God's favor—was taken away from him overnight. But why?

I hear from a lot of Christians who wonder the same thing about their lives. They walked happily in God's divine favor for years, but then suddenly things fell apart. Now they question everything: Did they really hear from the Lord? How did they miss His direction so badly? Will God be faithful to them despite it all?

David's response to these questions reveals everything.

The Bible tells us, "David encouraged himself in the Lord his God" (1 Samuel 30:6 kjv). David could have given in to discouragement. Instead, he kept his faith—and through his overwhelming trials, his faith continued to grow.

Friend, when your life takes a downturn and you're shivering in a dark cave, that's when your character is formed. For Paul, it was in prison; for David, it was in a cave. I found out something revealing about David's dark experiences as I was preparing this message. I studied his prayer life, and believe it or not, when things were going well for Israel's amazing young leader, the Bible doesn't record him praying. (David sang psalms, but worship is different from intimate, poured-out petition.) That changed during David's crisis. Inside the cave, he became a man of intense prayer.

142

Your dark cave is also where you find out who your friends are. While David was forced to hide out, word spread through Israel about his crisis. Suddenly, a lot of unlikely groups of people rallied around him. These were supporters whom David never would have expected. First of all, his estranged brothers came to his side in support. Then a group of experienced soldiers showed up to pledge their loyalty to David. These warriors weren't looking for more stripes on their sleeves; they came because they loved their leader and believed in his calling.

All of this reflects an incredible aspect of God's special favor: *As we endure our dark night, He works to reconcile our relationships.* You see, our Lord is more concerned about our relational losses than even we are. And beautiful restorations like David's might never have happened without his crisis.

After David emerged from the cave, we see a new spiritual authority in his life. Beginning with 1 Samuel 23, he moves in a supernatural power he hadn't known before. Yet it never would have happened without the divine shaping that comes through God's special favor.

Matthew's gospel contains a story that demonstrates the beauty of God's special favor in even the unlikeliest person's life. Matthew describes a scene in which a Canaanite woman approached Jesus in great need. Canaanites were Gentiles, meaning non-Jews. And in Jesus' day, the word *Gentile* pretty much meant "heathen"—meaning unclean, worshiping false gods, far from the one true Lord.

If you were a faithful Jew, you stayed as far away from Gentiles as possible. You were forbidden to even go into the home of a Gentile, eat with them or have any kind of physical contact. And Canaanites were considered on the low end of the Gentile scale.

You can imagine the public scene as this Canaanite woman begged Jesus to help her daughter, who was tormented by a demon.

> And behold, a Canaanite woman from that region came out and was crying, "Have mercy on me, O Lord, Son of David; my daughter is severely oppressed by a demon."
>
> Matthew 15:22 ESV

At first, Jesus responded as any righteous Jew of that time would. Scripture says, "But he did not answer her a word" (v. 23 ESV). The disciples' reaction was just as typical: "His disciples came and begged him, saying, 'Send her away, for she is crying out after us'" (v. 23 ESV). In short, the woman was causing a social scandal.

Surely this Canaanite woman knew the ruckus she was causing, but she didn't care. Now, I'm a grandparent, and if my grandkids were in dire need, as this woman's daughter was, I would make a scene, too, to get them the help they needed. To this woman, all that mattered was her daughter's need.

It must have been a heartbreaking story. I imagine her child growing up healthy and playing with her friends. Then one day, the little girl comes home from playing, and she has a horrid look on her face. Her menacing demeanor sends a chill through her mother, who knows something is desperately wrong.

In the coming days, her daughter begins to throw tormented fits. The fits grow worse and worse, frightening her siblings and causing her parents to panic. In public, the girl runs wild, alienating the family from everyone and causing neighbors to avoid them. Eventually, the family loses all hope. What once looked like God's favor in a blessed household has turned unimaginably dark, casting everyone into despair.

The gospels contain several stories of demon-possessed children and their desperate parents who came to Jesus hoping for a miracle. My heart breaks as I read these families' stories. They're living through the worst season of their lives. Their need is overwhelming, and they obviously turn to God's miracle-working power as their last hope. The Canaanite woman's story is all the more poignant because at her moment of deepest need, Jesus seems to turn His back on her: "He did not answer her a word" (v. 23 ESV).

Maybe you've felt what this mother did at that moment. Have you ever prayed to God in a time of raw, desperate need, but heaven seemed closed to you? You wonder what you did wrong that would cause the Lord to turn His ear from your cries. It can be devastating.

So how did this mother respond? She did what any tenacious mother would do: "She came and knelt before him, saying, 'Lord, help me'" (v. 25 ESV). But Jesus continued to seem to resist her: "He answered, 'I was sent only to the lost sheep of the house of Israel. . . . It is not right to take the children's bread and throw it to the dogs'" (vv. 24, 26 ESV).

No one at that scene knew it, but Jesus was setting up a teaching moment for all of Israel—and for us today. The point arrived with the determined woman's next response: "She said, 'Yes, Lord, yet even the dogs eat the crumbs that fall from their masters' table'" (v. 27 ESV).

Now Christ brought the lesson home: "Then Jesus answered her, 'O woman, great is your faith! Be it done for you as you desire.' And her daughter was healed instantly" (v. 28 ESV).

On one level, this is a deeply moving story of the compassion of our loving God. Yet it's much more than that. It's a story of God's special favor. This woman found God's favor not apart from struggles but in the midst of the most difficult struggle of her life. And the blessed, special favor she received was meant not just for her family but for all of Israel. Think about it: Jesus applauded a Canaanite woman for her great faith, when she wasn't even a part of the church. It was a lesson meant to open the eyes of God's people to how far-reaching His compassionate, healing grace goes.

Your dark season doesn't have to change
for you to know you're still in God's favor
and that He's working not just on your
behalf but for the sake of others, too.

Most of us pray for God to change our difficult circumstances. But if we knew the amazing work He's shaping in us and our world, we wouldn't want things to change at all. We would know the best is about to happen.

Remember my friend the worship musician, whom I described at the beginning of this chapter? As he walked faithfully through his pain, the Lord sent someone else into his life. She's an amazing Christian with a beautiful faith who was on her way to a top executive position with a firm in New York City. "She's out of my league," my friend confided to me as they dated. But she didn't think so. They got married, and he went on to become a leader in a major ministry. They're so happy today.

My friend thought he'd lost God's favor, but that wasn't the case at all. God worked through his tragic loss to design a blessing my friend never could have imagined. He cared about my friend's family life and restored it to him, just as he did with David. And everyone around him witnessed that blessing take shape.

Friend, that is the God who shows His children special favor. And He wants to bestow it on you in your crisis. So, don't despise your trial. I promise you, if you hold on to your faith, you'll know the depths of God's love as you never have. And you'll find your life—and perhaps others'—changed in amazing ways, marked by His compassionate, supernatural love.

11

Ultimate Favor

Knowing the Fullness of God's Awesome Favor

We've talked about the various dimensions of God's favor throughout this book. Now it's time to conclude with one last dimension that transcends all others. As you'll discover, I've saved the best for last. I call this dimension God's ultimate favor.

In an earlier chapter I talked about the biblical concept of a promised land. It's the arrival place for anyone seeking freedom, relief from bondage, and the joy of a blessed life. The original Promised Land was a gift God gave to ancient Israel, a literal place called Canaan, a fertile land bursting with oversized fruit and flowing rivers. It was the stuff of dreams for the Israelites. They'd been beaten down and exiled for generations, and yet when they arrived at Canaan's border—a land of plenty in every sense—God made an unusual statement to Moses: "Go up to a land flowing with milk and honey; but I will not go up among you, lest I consume you on the way, for you are a stiff-necked people" (Exodus 33:3 ESV).

What a shocker. God's message to His people here may sound harsh, but when it's put into context we see it's anything but that. The Lord had freed Israel from four hundred years of slavery in Egypt. Now, on the cusp of their entry into the Promised Land, He made this surprising declaration: "I will not go with you."

He explains why in the next phrase: "For you are a stiff-necked people." Even after all the miraculous things God did for the Israelites, they complained every time they faced a new hardship. Their experiences—and the miracles He performed for them—never translated into faith. Instead, the people attacked His character. They accused God of delivering them just to see them die in the desert. Every time Moses turned around, it seemed, they were threatening to reject God and abandon His leading.

But Moses' faith was different. He knew the goodness of God, recounting all of the Lord's supernatural works for Israel. In fact, to Moses, God's favor toward His people seemed bottomless, never-ending, unlimited. No matter what obstacle they faced or how impossible it seemed, God brought them through every time.

Moses marveled at the character of a God who would mercifully perform all these things on their behalf. So now, when the Lord said He wouldn't go with them into the Promised Land, Moses answered, "If your presence will not go with me, do not bring us up from here" (v. 15 ESV). In other words, "Lord, if You won't be there, then I'm not going."

Moses discerned the difference between God's *unlimited* favor and His *ultimate* favor.

Moses knew how important God's blessings were to Israel. His supernatural works had saved their lives. He sent manna from heaven when the people faced starvation. He brought water from a rock when their bodies were parched beyond their limits. Yet Moses recognized that even those vital blessings weren't the point of these experiences. Rather, it was to know and trust the compassionate, loving God who bestowed them.

Given this, Moses' next statement comes as no surprise: "Please show me now your ways, that I may know you in order to find favor in your sight" (v. 13 ESV). Moses knew that, ultimately, God's favor wasn't found in the blessings He provided; they were found in knowing the Lord Himself.

I thank God for all His earthly blessings. As a pastor, I get to see His amazing work in people's lives all the time. He restores marriages that have split apart. He provides for those who struggle financially. He brings healing to people's sick, broken bodies.

As I write this, I think of a little boy named Isaiah who wasn't expected to live for ten days after his birth. After he survived the first year, doctors said he'd never walk. Recently his mom sent me a video of young Isaiah dancing with a little girl at a wedding. I also think of a young man named Chad who was beaten down by the people meant to nurture him. The circumstances Chad faced in life were unbelievably hard. Yet now Chad is catching on to how much God loves him, and he wants to be baptized.

All of these things speak of God's unlimited favor—His ability to breathe life into any desert wilderness. We all experience His favor in ways too great to measure: our relationships, our health, our work, our studies. When we struggle in any area of life or our circumstances get too difficult, He s us with His soothing presence. God has done things ives we never could imagine happening. His unlimited favor knows no boundaries.

Yet Moses knew of something from the Lord that exceeded His unlimited blessings and even His supernatural works. He knew that beyond God's unlimited favor is His ultimate favor.

This sort of favor isn't found in the things God does; it's found in the Lord Himself. As Moses said, in so many words, "Lord, what good are grapes and milk and honey—all the blessings of life—if You're not present?"

C. S. Lewis posed a similar question. He asked, in essence, "What if heaven were a place where you could have everything you wanted—where all your dreams would come true, every aspiration and desire would be made a reality—but God wasn't there? Would you want to go?"

It's a legitimate question for any Christian. Do we desire God's blessings apart from knowing Him, the Giver of all good things? Or, like Moses, would we rather have every blessing stripped away than to lose God's presence?

I don't take God's blessings lightly. And neither does His Word. There's hardly a book in the Bible that doesn't mention God's concern for the poor. Poverty affects every area of the world, and we're called specifically to supply food to the hungry, hope to the downcast and healing to the brokenhearted. But for those of us who know God's abundant blessings, Moses conveys something important: Even daily bread pales compared to knowing God. Moses' example calls us to experience a higher kind of favor.

It's not that Christians today aren't grateful for God's blessings. Our problem is that many of us stop there. We say, "Lord, Your unlimited favor is enough for me." But according to this passage, it *isn't* enough. We can be blessed with the most vibrant marriage, the most beautiful home, the most fulfilling job, and the greatest kids—but if Jesus isn't in the midst of them, what do we have?

Are we willing to declare with Moses, "Lord, if you're not there, I won't go"? If we are, God will answer us as He did Moses: "My presence will go with you, and *I will give you rest*" (33:14 ESV, emphasis added).

The Lord wanted to enter Canaan with Israel, but He couldn't abide their idolatry. Even after the Lord blessed them powerfully, the Israelites turned to idols. While Moses was communing with God in the mountains, the people melted down their jewelry and made a golden statue of a calf. We may not be able to relate to this kind of thing today, but the upshot is this: When you pursue God's blessings without seeking God Himself, you end up in idolatry because the focus of your pursuit is something earthen. As Paul says, "They exchanged the truth about God for a lie and worshiped and served the creature rather than the Creator" (Romans 1:25 ESV).

Thankfully, today most of us don't have to plead for water or bread. We can just turn on the tap or go to the grocery store. But we have golden idols of our own, things we seek apart from God: job success, financial security, material comfort. Those aren't bad things. They're great blessings. But if we want them more than we want God—if they become the focus of our life's pursuit—we've built an idol. And God will say to us, "Go ahead, pursue that. Enjoy it. But you won't find Me present in it, and therefore, your soul won't find rest."

I love Moses' response: "God, kill me in the desert before you lead me to someplace that you aren't." I pray Moses' cry leads to a similar one from Christ's church:

Lord, my life has been so blessed that I've let myself get misdirected. My eyes have been on Your unlimited favor, the blessings You give. I want something different. Let my life be defined by Your ultimate favor—to know You for who You are.

Is God enough for you? Does knowing the Lord satisfy you? Or is there anything that keeps you from it, an idol you've put before Him? His first commandment is, "You shall have no other gods before me" (Exodus 20:3 ESV).

Knowing God was sufficient for Moses. Rather than going to the Promised Land, he asked, "Please show me your glory" (Exodus 33:18 ESV). I can imagine God's pleasure at hearing this. Every earthly parent knows the constant pleading of her children's voices asking for things, but nothing warms a mom's heart like hearing her child say, "Mommy, I love you for who you are."

God was so pleased with Moses' desire that He granted his request, as far as He could allow it. He replied, "You cannot see my face, for man shall not see me and live" (v. 20 ESV). God's unapproachable light is too fierce for humans to experience fully. His holiness is all consuming ("lest I consume you on the way," v. 3 ESV). But He did want Moses to experience His glory in part. The Lord told him, in effect, "I can't show you My face. But I can show you the effects of My presence and the trail of goodness I leave behind" (see vv. 21–23).

To protect Moses, He said, "While my glory passes by I will *put you in a cleft of the rock* . . . until I have passed by" (v. 22 ESV, emphasis added). This verse tells us everything about God's amazing grace in the Old Testament. Even before the cross—before Christ shed His blood for our salvation—

God hid Moses in His grace "in the crevice of the rock." As Paul explains, "the Rock was Christ" (1 Corinthians 10:4 ESV).

Scripture says Moses' face was transformed by God's glory. The impact was so powerful he had to "put a veil over his face so that the Israelites might not gaze at the outcome" (2 Corinthians 3:13 ESV). Anyone who encounters Jesus experiences the same transformation, a change so profound the whole world sees it and is awed.

Today God has removed every limitation and barrier to reveal the fullness of His glory in Jesus.

We all, with unveiled face, beholding the glory of the Lord, are being transformed into the same image from one degree of glory to another. For this comes from the Lord who is the Spirit.

2 Corinthians 3:18 ESV

These days we don't have to hide in a crevice as Moses did, because God's glory has been revealed fully in Jesus. We don't have to wait for water to be poured from a rock. Instead, rivers of living water flow to us continually from His indwelling Spirit.

God's ultimate favor isn't in a house or car or job. It's in His presence, and He doesn't withhold it from us. Christ's saving sacrifice has lifted the veil completely so we can know His glory without hindrance. That is God's supreme, ultimate favor!

The Israelites could have experienced God's glory, just as Moses did. The Lord wanted to accompany them into the Promised Land, but their bitterness prevented it. It had happened before. When they were without water in the wilderness, they put God on trial. The original Hebrew language suggests a hammer or gavel, meaning they judged the Lord and convicted Him.

What a horrible act, especially for a people so blessed by God. At a time when they could have trusted Him in faith, they complained, "At least in Egypt we had food and water. We had safety and security. We had homes to live in." Now that those things were taken away, the people were consumed with bitterness. Their idols had overcome them.

The same thing can happen to us today. How often does this describe our hearts toward God in our times of struggle? We're taken aback by our trial. A subtle anger can start to boil—and a shift in our heart occurs. Without knowing it, our focus can move from the Giver of blessings to the blessings that have been removed. We set our sights on getting them back, not on the One who gave them to us so graciously in the first place. And so, a cycle of subtle but undeniable idolatry begins: "God isn't coming through for me now. He isn't doing what He once did for me. He isn't meeting the longing in my heart."

Friend, you don't know it, but your trial is an act of mercy by your loving God. He's using your time of struggle to show you your heart's condition. As He holds up the mirror to you, what does your heart show you? Do you see yourself pursuing comfort in Him, the Giver of all good things—or in the things you're missing? Has your focus shifted from the God of all comfort to a possession or a person? An ambition or a goal?

What's God's response to us in these times? *He always offers mercy.* Here was God's mercy to the Israelites: Despite their sin of outright anger, God told Moses to strike a rock with his staff—and water came flowing out. Think about the incredible symbolism of this scene. God was telling Moses, "Don't strike the people. I don't want them destroyed over this. Strike the rock instead." That rock represented Jesus. It bore the brunt of God's wrath for His people's sins. And what came out of the rock when it was struck? Living water: "For they drank from the spiritual Rock that followed them, and the Rock was Christ" (1 Corinthians 10:4 ESV).

Friend, the Rock that is Jesus Christ is always there for you. He is your Rock in the wilderness, just as He was for Israel. And just like then, He is unmovable in His ability to bear your sins. Best of all, His living water is sufficient for you in every situation.

Consider all He has done. He has removed every curse and given you blessing instead. His favor follows you, while always before you is His season of increase. His continual presence with you gives you power to conquer cynicism and to take bold, courageous stands to change your family's destiny. His Spirit causes you to raise your sights to overwhelming victories, because He is glad to supply you with all you need for every situation.

He empowers you to proclaim and to show His favor, changing others' worlds. He shows you His special favor by empowering you to face difficulties, all meant to lead you to a higher calling. And, finally, He calls you to know His awesome favor in its fullness by knowing Him.

I have one final question for you: What does your heart long for?

Is your main dream a financial one, a material desire? Or, can you say your heart's desire is the hope of God's glory, which transforms all of life? He has blessed you abundantly with the unlimited favor of His blessings. Yet there's more to know of our great God than earthly blessings. He wants you to know His glorious presence in every realm of life.

Like Moses, we're able to know something of God that exceeds even His supernatural blessings. And in order to mature in faith as He desires for us, we need to make a shift in our hearts from seeking His *unlimited* favor to seeking His *ultimate* favor.

If you want to make that shift, then pray with me:

Lord, show me every idol that prevents me from Your presence. Don't let anything—even the good things you've blessed me with—blind me to You in any way. I won't go anywhere or do anything if You're not there. I want to know Your presence in the midst of everything. You're all I need.

Today is a new season in your walk with the Lord—a season of unlimited, ultimate favor that will be marked by the power and presence of God. Your life will never be the same.

Gary Wilkerson's passionate desire is to help people lead a better life and make a better world. He pursues this through creative writing, blogs, podcasts, YouTube videos, books and leadership conferences he has held in over sixty nations, touching tens of thousands of activists, pastors, politicians, social workers, missionaries, leaders and change agents. He believes God designed us to live for something bigger than ourselves, and that love should be our greatest ambition. He brings this message through a newsletter touching 250,000 people monthly and social media encouraging thousands daily.

He is the president of World Challenge, which brings poverty solutions within reach for some of the poorest communities in the world, and helps people live out their highest calling and fulfill their God-designed destinies. Gary is an avid CrossFit workout enthusiast and health food aficionado. He is blessed with an amazing wife, Kelly, and four children, who are all making a better world in their own way.